MARGARET LAURENCE

THE DIVINERS

NOTES

COLES EDITORIAL BOARD

Bound to stay open

Publisher's Note

Otabind (Ota-bind). This book has been bound using the patented Otabind process. You can open this book at any page, gently run your finger down the spine, and the pages will lie flat.

ABOUT COLES NOTES

COLES NOTES have been an indispensible aid to students on five continents since 1948.

COLES NOTES are available for a wide range of individual literary works. Clear, concise explanations and insights are provided along with interesting interpretations and evaluations.

Proper use of COLES NOTES will allow the student to pay greater attention to lectures and spend less time taking notes. This will result in a broader understanding of the work being studied and will free the student for increased participation in discussions.

COLES NOTES are an invaluable aid for review and exam preparation as well as an invitation to explore different interpretive paths.

COLES NOTES are written by experts in their fields. It should be noted that any literary judgement expressed herein is just that – the judgement of one school of thought. Interpretations that diverge from, or totally disagree with any criticism may be equally valid.

COLES NOTES are designed to supplement the text and are not intended as a substitute for reading the text itself. Use of the NOTES will serve not only to clarify the work being studied, but should enhance the readers enjoyment of the topic.

ISBN 0-7740-3489-0

© COPYRIGHT 1998 AND PUBLISHED BY
COLES PUBLISHING COMPANY
TORONTO - CANADA
PRINTED IN CANADA

Manufactured by Webcom Limited
Cover finish: Webcom's Exclusive **DURACOAT**

CONTENTS

Margaret Laurence: Life and Works

> We stand in need of our gods, and we need links with
> our ancestors, partly in order to determine who and
> what we are, to decide what we hope to become, and
> to know what sort of a society we will try to form. Fic-
> tion . . . both binds us to and frees us from our ances-
> tors; it acknowledges our dilemmas; it mourns and
> rages at our inhumanity to one another; and some-
> times it expresses our faith in growth and change, and
> honours our children and our faith in them.

These words of Margaret Laurence serve well as an introduction to one of Canada's finest and foremost writers. We discover in Laurence a profound sense of continuity between past
and future, and a keen awareness of our present gifts. She was
born Jean Margaret Wemyss on July 18, 1926, in Neepawa — a
small prairie town north-west of Winnipeg, Manitoba. Her
roots on her mother's side are Irish-Canadian: her maternal
grandfather, John Simpson, was a stern, domineering man — a
cabinet-maker and undertaker — who settled in Neepawa in the
late 1880s. On her father's side, the ancestry is Scottish-Canadian: Grandfather Wemyss, a Lowland Scot, was the lawyer
responsible for incorporating the town of Neepawa in 1883.

When Laurence was four years old, her mother died suddenly. Aunt Margaret Simpson came to look after the child and
subsequently married young Margaret's father. A son, Robert,
was born in 1933. Two years later, both Margaret's father and
her Grandmother Simpson died. Grandfather Simpson's brick
house became home for Margaret and her half-brother when, in
1938, her step-mother was forced by financial hardship to move
into it.

Encouraged by her step-mother, Laurence started writing
in notebooks at the age of 6 or 7. When she was 12, one of her
poems was published in the *Winnipeg Free Press*. A year later,
the same paper published her short story, "Pillars of the
Nation," in which she first used the name "Manawaka" for her
fictionalized Neepawa.

After attending Neepawa College and editing the school
paper, Laurence entered United College (now the University of
Winnipeg) on a scholarship. She majored in English, began a

1

life-long friendship with a fellow-writer Adele Wiseman, and became involved with socialism in the Winnipeg Old Left. She graduated with honours in 1947 and subsequently worked as a labour reporter and a book reviewer for the *Winnipeg Citizen*. A year later, Margaret married fellow-Manitoban Jack Laurence, a civil engineer. The next year they moved to England.

The Laurences spent 1950-1952 in the British East African Protectorate of Somaliland, where Jack was in charge of constructing dams and reservoirs. Laurence began collecting Somali poems and stories, which she translated, and which the Somali government published in 1954 as *A Tree of Poverty*. This was Laurence's first book. Three more books came out of her experiences in Africa: in 1954, Laurence began writing *The Tomorrow Tamer*; and in 1957 she began the novel entitled *This Side Jordan*. *The Prophet's Camel Bell*, also about Africa, was published in 1963.

In Africa, Laurence matured as a person and as a writer. There she refined her skills as a wordsmith, learned how to listen for the particular voices which would individualize her characters and realized values which would echo throughout all of her writings.

After leaving Somaliland, the Laurences travelled to England and then moved to the West African British colony of the Gold Coast, where they lived from 1952 until 1957. Two children were born during this time. The family then moved to Vancouver. Here, Laurence wrote the first draft of her first Manawaka novel — *The Stone Angel*.

In 1962, Laurence separated amicably from her husband and moved with the children to England. There she worked on a second draft of *The Stone Angel*, composed the Vanessa MacLeod stories later collected in *A Bird in the House* and wrote numerous book reviews. She moved, in 1964, from Hampstead, London, to Elm Cottage — a delightful retreat in the Buckinghamshire countryside. This move coincided with the publication in Canada, the United States and England of *The Stone Angel*.

The Stone Angel was not intended to set off what are now called the Manawaka Books, but it did. It must be noted that the five books set in Manawaka are neither a series nor a number of sequels. They are related only by the fact that many of the characters in these books live, or have lived, in the fictional community of Manawaka.

Laurence began the third of these books, *The Fire-Dwellers*, in 1966. At this time, *A Jest of God* was published, for which she won the Governor-General's Medal for Fiction (Paul Newman purchased the film rights for the book, and produced and directed the film version, which was entitled *Rachel, Rachel*). That same year, Laurence was made an Honorary Fellow of her *alma mater*, United College — the first of many academic honours that would come her way.

More recognition followed: Laurence was appointed Writer-in-Residence at Massey College, University of Toronto in 1969-1970; in 1971 she was made a Companion of the Order of Canada — the nation's highest honour. Trent University awarded her an honorary Doctor of Laws degree in 1972 and later (1974) she served there as Writer-in-Residence. In 1975 Laurence won a second Governor-General's Medal for Fiction for *The Diviners*.

Much of *The Diviners* was written during the summers of 1971-1973 which Laurence spent at a cottage on the Otonabee River, near Peterborough, Ontario. The property, bought after her divorce in 1969, was named "Manawaka." Then, when Laurence sold her English residence in 1974 to return to Canada permanently, she settled in a yellow-brick Victorian house (similar to her Grandfather Simpson's home) located near her Manawaka cottage in the village of Lakefield.

Laurence felt that *The Diviners* would be her last novel. But she continues to write essays; book reviews and children's literature: *The Heart of a Stranger*, a book of essays compiled from various writings of the sixties and seventies, and published in 1976, gives many insights into the writer's craft and values. Her first children's book — *Jason's Quest*, came out in 1970. *Six Darn Cows* and *The Christmas Birthday Story* are both books for the very young. *The Olden Days Coat* (published in 1979 and made into an award-winning CBC film in 1981) is a charming tale about a young girl, resentful of spending Christmas with her grandmother, who is magically taken back into the past. There she meets and becomes friends with her grandmother — as a girl. The tale reveals the power of the imagination in bringing us closer to others through empathy and love.

In recent years Laurence has also given many interviews and written many letters to the newspapers. She considers nuclear war and pollution two of the gravest dangers facing

3

humanity. In 1983 she wrote the Foreword to *Canada and the Nuclear Arms Race*.

What she writes in that foreword relates to concerns shown less explicitly and less personally in her novels. Arguing for Canada becoming a nuclear-free zone, she warns against giving way to despair: "We cannot afford passivity," she writes, "We must take responsibility for our lives and our world, and be prepared to make our government listen and act. To do this, we must be informed." Why? Her answer should not come as a surprise. "If we will not speak for our children," she writes, "if we will not speak out for the survival of our own land and our wider home Earth, in God's name what will move us?"

List of Works

Translations
A Tree for Poverty: Somali Poetry and Prose	1954

Travel
The Prophet's Camel Bell	1963

Short Stories
The Tomorrow Tamer	1963
A Bird in the House	1970

Criticism
Long Drums and Cannons: Nigerian Dramatists and Novelists 1952-1966	1968

Essays
Heart of a Stranger	1976

Children's Stories
Jason's Quest	1970
The Olden Days Coat	1979
Six Darn Cows	1979
The Christmas Birthday Story	1980

Novels
This Side Jordan	1960
The Stone Angel	1964
A Jest of God	1966
The Fire-Dwellers	1969
The Diviners	1974

4

Introduction to *The Diviners*

"A title should, if possible, be like a line of poetry — capable of saying a great deal with hardly any words," writes Margaret Laurence in *The Heart of a Stranger*. She adds that a title should in some way suggest the whole novel — its themes, even some of its outcome.

The Diviners is aptly titled. When we come to the last of the five parts which comprise the novel, we find the same title is applied to the closing section of the work. By that time we have a better appreciation of its value than we had at the beginning of the book.

The meaning of the word, and the tribe of words to which it belongs, must be considered. *Divine* can be a noun, an adjective or a verb. As a noun, *diviner* describes a religious person, coming as it does from the Latin *divus*, meaning *god*. As an adjective, *divine* means: having the nature of a deity or god; being the expression of the divine, of God; sacred, holy; in the service of a god or God; or superhuman, godly. Finally, the verb *to divine* means "to foretell the future or the unknown through the art of divination; to know through inspiration, intuition, or reflection; to guess." In all of the above, the important thing to note is the connection of the word with God. To be a diviner is to have insight into what is essential, yet invisible to the eye.

In the literal sense of the word, Royland is a diviner — one who uses a rod to dowse or find underground sources of water which can then be drilled for wells. But the novel is not entitled *The Diviner*. The noun is significantly plural. By the end of the book, it is clear that several characters are diviners: Christie, Jules, Dan McRaith, Pique, Morag herself — all are diviners in their own right.

Through her association with Royland Morag grows to understand the nature of divining. She is fascinated by the magical power of the divining rod. However, when she tries to use it herself, nothing happens. Royland tells her she does not have the gift or talent for using a willow wand. "She wasn't surprised," we are told. "Her area was elsewhere . . . ." Morag eventually realizes that both she and Royland are diviners, but in different ways. Her medium is words and writing.

Morag acknowledges that her first diviner was Christie Logan. She tells Ella that "Christie knew things about inner truths that I am only just beginning to understand." Christie — note the connection with Christ suggested by his name — was the one who divined his knowledge of people by scavenging through the garbage of Manawaka. Additionally, his "scavenging" through literature and legend enables him to realize the power of the past to help shape and give meaning to our lives. Christie's tales transport Morag into the past of her people, into the myths that eventually become quite real to her. Through Christie's tales — through knowledge of her past — Morag first divines what she must do as her mission in life.

Jules is another diviner. His tales of the Métis heritage, which mingle with the stories and memories instilled in Morag, are passed on by her to their daughter, Pique. Pique is born to divine also. Music is her medium: she goes back to her roots, her French-Cree past, and recreates that past in her songs.

At the end of the novel, Royland calmly accepts that the gift of divining has been withdrawn from him, to be given to someone else. He reveals in the last pages of the novel that A-Okay can *learn* to divine water. This is important, because ultimately we must recognize that we too can become diviners. Through faith and work we can begin to divine truths about our lives. This, perhaps, is the gift that Margaret Laurence offers her readers in this novel.

Jamie Halpern: Fellow-pupil of Morag in Manawaka Public School.

Harold: Vancouver newscaster, separated from his wife, who picks up Morag at a literary party. After two sexual encounters, she finds him boring and starts to feel sorry for his wife.

Hector Jonas: Funeral director of the Japonica Chapel in Manawaka in the 1960s. Despite his slick manner, Morag finds him genuinely kind and solicitous when she comes to make arrangements for Christie's funeral.

Julie Kazlik: Fellow-pupil of Morag in Manawaka. In her teens she has many boyfriends; in her late twenties she is disillusioned and seeks only kindness. She contacts Morag after reading her articles in a Vancouver newspaper. Despite the breakdown of her marriage to the impotent Buckle Fennick, she is not defeated. She plans to remarry and move with her son, Steve, to Montreal.

Mike Lobodiak: Fellow-pupil of Morag in Manawaka and Julie Kazlik's teenaged boyfriend.

Christie Logan: "Tough, wiry, and proud as the devil," he is the Manawaka garbageman who takes the orphaned Morag into his home. His stories of the past thrill Morag's imagination and inspire her to become a writer. As a teenager, she rejects him out of shame, but later comes to recognize him as her "real" father and first diviner.

Princess Logan (Prin): Christie's wife and Morag's substitute mother. Addicted to jelly doughnuts, she is grotesquely fat, a whiner, and not very bright, but she looks after Morag as best she can. She becomes prematurely senile and dies after a long period as an invalid.

Lachlan MacLachlan: Editor and owner of *The Manawaka Banner*. During World War II, Morag is his sole reporter. When his son, Dave, is killed at Dieppe, Lachlan is devastated. Later he commits suicide.

Dr. Ewen MacLeod: Admired doctor in Manawaka, he attends to Colin and Louisa Gunn in their final illness. Father of Vanessa, he dies when she is in Grade Six.

Vanessa MacLeod: Fellow-pupil of Morag in Manawaka. (She is the narrator and main character in Laurence's semi-autobiographical short story collection *A Bird in the House*.)

Clowny MacPherson: Hero of one of Morag's first childhood stories about her past. Morag conceives him as a strong, scrawny little man whom people laugh at, but who is much respected by Piper Gunn.

Jock MacRae: Printer of *The Manawaka Banner*, he teaches Morag proofreading and layout.

Hank Masterson: Middle-aged Vancouver representative of the publishing house, Walton & Pierce. He gives Morag royalties from her first novel, gets her an agent, and encourages her to keep writing.

Mrs. McKee: Wife of the Reverend McKee the United Church minister, she is Morag's Sunday School teacher whose insistence that "God is love" offends the recently orphaned girl. Morag, to her later regret, shows her first poetry to Mrs. McKee.

Mr. McKendrick: Farmer near Freehold, Manitoba, who marries Eva Winkler, knowing she has had an abortion and is now sterile.

Miss McMurtrie: Grade Six teacher at Manawaka Public School. She recognizes Morag's intelligence.

Bridget McRaith (Bridie): Wife of Dan and mother of seven children, she lives in her native village of Crombruach in the Scottish Highlands. A good woman, she is shy and passive and presents no stimulus to her husband. Morag realizes that Bridie's constancy is just what Dan needs.

Dan McRaith: Scottish painter in his mid-forties whose sexuality attracts Morag on their first meeting. His free artistic spirit wins her respect and, after becoming lovers, they also remain close friends. They see each other irregularly over a period of three years.

Archie McVitie: Manawaka lawyer in partnership with Simon Pearl

Mrs. McVitie: Wife of Archie McVitie and mother of Ross, she is a small-minded, snobbish woman.

Ross McVitie: Fellow-pupil of Morag in Manawaka. She considers him "an ignorant slob."

Miss Melrose: Morag's adored Grade Nine English teacher, she is the first person to encourage and to criticize Morag's writing.

Mort: We never learn his last name, but he is Ella Gerson's second husband.

Rufus Nolan: Manawaka policeman.

Mr. Parsons: Owner of the bakery in Manawaka.

Nurse Patterson: Head nurse at the Manawaka Hospital when Christie is dying.

Henry Pearl: Colin Gunn's neighbour. He sells some of the Gunn property before creditors get to it so he can set up a trust fund for Morag's future education.

Mrs. Pearl: Wife of Henry, she looks after Morag while Colin and Louisa Gunn are dying.

Simon Pearl: Manawaka lawyer, son of Henry Pearl. When Jules is in high school he boards with Simon and his wife.

Young Mrs. Pearl: Never identified by a first name, she is called Young Mrs. Pearl to distinguish her from her mother-in-law.

Miss Plowright: One of Morag's teachers in public school, she suspects Morag is "not all there."

Royland: 74-years old, he is Morag's neighbour near McConnell's Landing and a water-diviner. Morag always senses she has something to learn from him.

Jeremy Sampson: Elderly Englishman, lover of the contemporary novel and owner of the Agonistes Bookshop in London. He gives Morag a job as his assistant.

Dan Scranton: Young Westerner who gets involved with Pique at McConnell's Landing. He admits to being "too anxious" to have people like him. Morag helps him realize that he cannot entirely reject his past and the father he has rebelled against.

John Shipley: Son of Hagar Shipley in *The Stone Angel*. Before his death in a head-on collision in the 1930s, he had traded Lazarus a plaid pin from his mother's forebears in exchange for a knife. Through a strange set of circumstances, the knife and the pin come down to Morag and Jules and, eventually, to Pique.

Anne Skelton: Brooke's second wife, who is even younger than Morag. Anne is smart, well-dressed and apparently quite content to be subordinate to her husband.

Brooke Skelton: Morag's first-year English professor at university and, within the year, her husband. For ten years he patronizes and criticizes her, but refuses to father the child Morag wants. After her first novel is published, Morag leaves him.

Alf Smith (A-Okay): Husband of Maude and father of Tom, he is Morag's unofficial protector at McConnell's Landing. A liberal back-to-the-land person who has fled computer-programming teaching in Toronto, he becomes a would-be poet, new pioneer, horse-raiser and writer of popular science articles.

Maude Smith (Maudie): Wife of A-Okay and mother of Tom, she is a young, liberated woman who is immensely support-ive of A-Okay.

Tom Smith: Precocious young son of A-Okay and Maudie.

Ina Spettigue: As a Manawaka teenager during World War II, she is a favourite with the soldiers.

Mr. Tate: Teacher at Manawaka Public School.

Maggie Tefler: Frizzy-haired, fortyish landlady of the Bleak House in Kitsilano where Morag stays when she first comes to Vancouver. She takes advantage of Morag's pregnancy and poverty by having her do all the housework and then insults and abuses her verbally.

Tiny: Dancing partner of Fan Brady, he is a beautiful brown and cream python. When he dies, Fan is heart-broken.

Rider Tonnerre (Chevalier): Ancestor of Jules (Skinner) Ton-nerre, his stories come down to Jules through Jules' father, Lazarus. As the Prince of the Braves, Rider Tonnerre led the Métis against the English and Scottish settlers at the Red River Colony; as an old man, he shamed his people into supporting Louis Riel.

Jacques Tonnerre: Younger brother of Jules (Skinner). As a man, he and his wife Mary settle at Galloping Mountain where they bring up their own children along with other or-phaned or abandoned Métis.

Jules Tonnerre: Grandfather of Jules (Skinner). At the age of eighteen, he was in the North-West Rebellion of 1885 with Louis Riel. After the defeat, he lost his spirit.

Jules Tonnerre (Skinner): Métis, three years older than Morag, he becomes her first lover and later fathers Pique. Until his premature death at 51 years of age, he moves in and out of Morag's life, never staying for long.

Lazarus Tonnerre: Father of Jules, Piquette, Valentine, Jacques and Paul. When Morag meets him he is 39, but looks twice his age. Lazarus instills pride into his sons with tales of the Métis people and their past.

Mary Tonnerre: Wife of Jacques.

Paul Tonnerre: Youngest brother of Jules, he becomes a tourist guide in Northern Manitoba. When he drowns at the age of 25, Jules suspects foul play.

Piquette Tonnerre: Sister of Jules, Jacques, Paul and Valentine, she contracts tuberculosis, drops out of school, marries Al Cummings and moves to Winnipeg. After Al deserts her, she moves with her two children back to the Tonnerre shacks in the Wachakwa Valley outside Manawaka, where she takes to drinking heavily. She and her children are burned to death when the shack catches fire in the winter of 1942.

Valentine Tonnerre: Younger sister of Jules. She drifts to the West Coast where she becomes a prostitute and alcoholic and eventually dies.

Catharine Parr Traill: (1802-1899) Sister of Susanna Moodie, English settler and pioneer in the bush country near Peterborough, Ontario in the 1830s. The author of many books and guides about pioneer life, she inspires and intimidates Morag, who imaginatively adopts her as a mentor.

Eva Winkler: Fellow-pupil of Morag and her best friend in the Manawaka years. Eva fails and falls behind in school, becomes pregnant, has an abortion, and drops out of school. Morag is determined not to become "beaten by life" like Eva.

Gus Winkler: Brutal father of Eva and Vernon, he has "a devil in him" according to Prin Logan.

Mrs. Winkler: Battered wife of Gus.

Vernon Winkler: As a boy in Manawaka, he is small, timid, and frequently beaten by his father. As a man, he leaves Manawaka for Vancouver (where he becomes the glamorous, silver-haired supersalesman, Thor Thorlakson, in *The Fire-Dwellers*).

Plot Summary

The Diviners is a complex novel, an interweaving of many coloured and textured threads to form an intricate tapestry. Much of what happens involves little physical action. Indeed, most of the "action" of the novel occurs within the mind of its chief character, Morag Gunn. In the realms of thought, imagination and memory, Morag is seeking to divine the meaning of her experience — an experience which is not the experience of one lifetime only. The connections between Morag and her past go back and forth in the shuttle of her mind until, in the concluding chapter, she is able to bring them all together in her understanding.

Two time frameworks exist in the novel. The first takes us from the beginning of summer to the fall of a year in the early 1970s. The second takes us chronologically through Morag's life as projected through a series of snapshots and memorybank movies in Morag's head. In the final chapter, these two timeframes have woven together.

Morag grows up in Manawaka, a small Manitoba town. She is orphaned as a child. Christie and Prin Logan take her in and raise her until she leaves for Winnipeg and university after World War II.

Christie is the town garbageman, or "Scavenger," as he is called to Morag's dismay. He and Prin are poor, but they do their best for Morag as she goes through school during the Depression years of the 1930s.

It is Christie who gives Morag a sense of pride in her past and in herself by telling her stories of her mythical ancestors, Piper and Morag Gunn, and of the heroic deeds of her father in World War I. These tales inspire Morag to start creating her own stories, which she writes in her notebook.

Morag frequently feels herself an outsider in Manawaka. Many of the children in the school scorn her. She is ashamed of her poverty and embarrassed by Christie and Prin. She soon recognizes a silent ally in Jules "Skinner" Tonnerre, a Métis youth in her school. They walk and talk by the Wachakwa River and eventually she has her first sexual experience with him. He moves in and out of her life, never staying for long. He tells her other stories — tales he has heard from his drunken father, Lazarus, about the Indian and Métis past of the prairies. These

14

stories are different from the tales told by Christie, or the accounts found in history books in that they express a different vision of the past. Morag is struck by the realization that there is no single version of the truth, but rather, many truths. While her whole life, in one sense, is a search for what *really* happened, she will come at last to claim the myths to be her reality.

Jules leaves school and joins the army. For several years Morag does not hear from him — a pattern that is repeated throughout their lives. She completes high school and goes to work for the *Manawaka Banner* as a reporter. It is in this capacity that she witnesses the fire in which Jules' sister, Piquette, and her two children are burned to death.

This experience sickens Morag. She determines to leave Manawaka forever. Heroism such as exists in Christie's stories no longer impresses her. Christie and Manawaka represent everything she must escape. After one brief meeting with Jules after the war, she escapes to Winnipeg and university. She vows she will never return to Manawaka.

Morag is liberated by university. She forms a life-long friendship with a young poet named Ella Gerson. She also meets Dr. Brooke Skelton, her first-year English professor. Swept off her feet by this "prince among men," she leaves university to marry him and to relocate in Toronto where he has a new appointment. Over the next few years, Morag subordinates herself to a man who condescends to her, treating her as a child. Morag writes her first novel while married to Brooke, but he fails to take her seriously as an adult or as a writer. Her growing independence frightens him; the thought that she might succeed without him is a threat to his self-image.

One day Morag meets Jules on the street and brings him home for dinner. After Brooke insults him, Morag leaves with Jules. She lives with him for three weeks in a rooming house. At this time, she intentionally becomes pregnant. When Jules accuses her of using him to break the spell of Brooke, she cannot argue. She tells her husband their marriage is over, and takes the train to Vancouver. There she hopes to give birth to her child and live off the royalties from her first novel.

Jules and Morag understand that they will make no demands on each other. Their daughter, Pique, is born in Vancouver and named after Jules' sister who died in the terrible fire. Little Pique is brought up by Morag alone, first in Vancouver, then in England, and later near McConnell's Landing in Southern Ontario. Morag drifts from place to place in search of a home, which she finally realizes she must make for herself in Canada. She is also searching for her identity as a woman, mother and writer, and as an individual in a community. Jules never does find a home; he is also a creator, a roving balladeer who can never tell his own story. Occasionally and briefly Morag and Jules drift back into each other's lives, their connection never truly broken by either space or time.

In England, Morag finds a spiritual and sexual partner in Dan McRaith, a married Scottish painter who must periodically leave his remote village of Crombruach in the Highlands to come to London. He and Morag become lovers and friends, but they can never be together for long.

When Morag and Pique go to visit Dan and his family in Crombruach, Morag acknowledges that although Scotland may be the home of her ancestors, it is not *her* home. In spite of her vow never to return to Manawaka, she realizes that she must return to the place she thought she had left behind, but which has always been within her. "The myths are my reality," she affirms. Christie's land is her land, the land he has helped create for, and with, her. When she learns that he is dying, she returns home — to Canada. There she admits to Christie, before he dies, that he has been a real father to her.

After visiting Ella at her home in Toronto, Morag eventually buys an old farm in Southern Ontario. There she will make her home. Now in early middle age, she is an established writer, but writing is no easier than before. She is also a single woman with a growing daughter whose own identity must be respected. While Morag has told Pique of her double heritage, Pique must come to terms with her past herself. Morag is now the parent who must be rebelled against, and, although Morag understands, it is not easy for her to let go.

Throughout this long summer by the river, Morag reminisces about her past, trying to divine the significance of her memories. She is also working on her latest and possibly last novel. Her neighbour, Royland, is a 74-year-old water diviner whose kindly nature and unfathomable gift for finding hidden sources of water are a constant amazement and inspiration to her. As the summer draws to an end, Jules dies by his own hand before the final onslaught of throat cancer; and Pique decides

16

she must strike out for Manitoba to make her songs and contribute to the Métis community at Galloping Mountain.

Morag herself has been in the habit of summoning up the ghost of Catharine Parr Traill, one of the area's early pioneers, and of having long conversations aloud with her. At first Mrs. Traill is awesome in her sense of order and in her strong sense of survival, and Morag defers to her fearsome authority. But by the end of the novel we see that Morag finally has the strength to dismiss her "Saint Catharine" and take responsibility for her own life.

Chapter by Chapter
Summaries and Commentaries

NOTE: All quotations are from Margaret Laurence's *The Diviners*. (Toronto: McClelland and Steward, New Canadian Library Edition, 1978.)

PART I • CHAPTER 1

Summary

As the novel opens, Morag Gunn, a 47-year-old writer, is gazing out the window of her house and watching the river flow by. It is a mid-June morning in the early 1970s. Morag has found a note stuck in her typewriter from her 18-year-old daughter, Pique, saying that she has left home to head out west. This turn of events excites mixed feelings in Morag: as a mother, she fears for her child; as a woman and a writer, she admires her. Pique has left home once before, and Morag is not made comfortable by memories of that bad time. But she reflects that she is lucky to be a novelist whose work can take her mind off her personal life.

Sipping coffee, gazing out the window and meditating, she observes her 74-year-old neighbour, Royland, fishing. Royland is a diviner who discovers underground sources of water. Morag always feels on the verge of learning from him "something of great significance . . . something which would explain everything."

Morag resumes thinking about Pique's departure for the west. What would Pique's father (Jules "Skinner" Tonnerre) think if he knew? Would Pique go to Manawaka, the small Manitoba town where Morag and Jules grew up? And, if she did, would she find anything meaningful there?

This last question impels Morag to get up and search for her envelope of old photographs. She finds them and sorts them out in chronological order, realizing that she needs them not for what they show, but for what is hidden in them. The rest of the chapter consists of descriptions of the snapshots and reflections on their hidden elements.

These snapshots move from the mid-1920s when Morag's parents, Colin and Louisa Gunn, stand in front of their farm gate, through the next few years, showing a generally serious

Morag at two, three, four and five. Morag does not remember the reality of these photos, only the later invented fantasies she attached to them, including her imaginary childhood friends.

Recalling her invisible childhood companions, Morag regrets that they — and the strange and marvellous experiences they had shared — are more real to her than are her parents. She wonders what kind of a character she herself is. These present ponderings move into the first ''Memorybank Movie'' which takes place in Morag's head. It is set in the continuing present tense and stars the young Morag growing up.

Old Mrs. Pearl from the neighbouring farm has come to look after Morag while her parents are ill. Morag is scared that something she doesn't understand is going on, and when Mrs. Pearl firmly prevents her from going upstairs to see her parents, she *knows* that something is very wrong. When Dr. MacLeod comes to the house, she neither speaks nor smiles and refuses to let on that anything is happening.

Several nights later, Morag hears a weird crying, like that of a coyote, which she recognizes as being her father's. No sound comes from her mother. Morag is terrified. Several days elapse before Mrs. Pearl tells Morag that her parents have ''passed on to a happier land.'' Morag knows that they are dead. She resents Mrs. Pearl's refusal to let her see her parents, who have died of polio. God is not good, she decides. The next day, Morag sneaks upstairs. Her parents are not there. The day before, her imaginary playmates deserted her forever. She is alone.

Mrs. Pearl tells Morag that, since she has no relatives near-by, she will be brought up by Christie and Prin Logan, a child-less couple in the nearby town of Manawaka. Christie is an old friend of Colin Gunn from their soldiering days in World War I. Despite Mrs. Pearl's assurances that the Logans are kind but poor, Morag is mute; she knows she cannot argue. And so she leaves the farm forever.

Morag's first inner movie fades out, and she is crying, even though she doesn't know for sure how much she remembers and how much she has imagined.

She does know, however, that her father's land, house, and possessions were sold to pay off the mortgage. Christie told her this years later. She also knows that Mr. Pearl had reserved several items out of the house to sell and had to put the proceeds into a bank account for her to use when she turned eighteen. She remembers that Christie once took her to visit her parents' grave in the Manawaka cemetery. She was eight or ten years old at the time, and she didn't want to go.

Now Morag wishes she could know what her parents were *really* like, but she has no way of knowing, nor does she understand why it should matter to her. All that remains of them are two sepia shadows on an old snapshot and dim memories she can barely recall. Perhaps, she wonders, she only wants their forgiveness for having forgotten them. Yet she knows that they continue to live inside her, "flowing unknown in my blood and moving unrecognized in my skull."

Commentary

The opening chapter of any novel demands much consideration from the reader. Although the opening and closing chapters of *The Diviners* are brief, they merit closer attention than the much longer intervening chapters.

Chapter 1 introduces the main character and partial narrator of the novel, Morag Gunn. Other important characters — Pique Tonnerre Gunn, Pique's father (Jules Tonnerre — unnamed until Chapter 3), Royland, Christie and Prin Logan — are introduced either directly or indirectly.

Morag is established as a watcher and a doer, an observer of life and a participant in it. As she dips back into her own past through her snapshots and her memorybank movies and relives them in the present, she tries to distinguish between what she remembers and what she has made up. She is not always able to decide, but she is always concerned with what is real, what is true. This concern will preoccupy her throughout her life.

The structure of the novel is set up in this first chapter. Part of this structure can be seen in the connection between the opening sentence and the last sentence of the chapter and the connection of them to the last paragraphs of the novel.

"The river flowed both ways." This, the first sentence of *The Diviners*, is a highly significant sentence and image. The image of the river and the idea of "flow" is sustained throughout the novel. Literally, the river is the river flowing southward to Lake Ontario and being rippled backwards by the southerly wind. Symbolically, the river suggests time and the mysterious processes of the mind. The paradox or seeming contradiction involved in the river's flowing both ways is continued throughout the book and culminates in the novel's third last paragraph: "Look ahead into the past, and back into the future, until the silence." This mystery may be seen as one of the themes of the novel. The last sentence of this chapter adds another sense to the paradox in that Morag's dead parents continue to flow unknown in her blood and move unrecognized in her mind.

Imaginatively, the river — unnamed by Laurence — may be seen as a character in the novel. It appears in each chapter.

Notes

Ophelia: Character in Shakespeare's *Hamlet*. After Hamlet rejects her, and her father dies, she goes mad and falls into a river where she drowns. (p. 3)

apocalypse: The last days; the end of the world. (See the Book of Revelation in The Bible.) (p. 4)

The Nuisance Grounds: The town dump of Manawaka. (p. 5)

totem: The symbol of a tribe, associated with one's ancestral spirits. (p. 6)

Sutherland: County in the far north of Scotland, ancestral home of the Gunns and the Logans. (p. 10)

The Highland Clearances: Series of violent events in the early 1800s, during which the peasants of the Scottish Highlands were dispossessed of their lands by the English. (p. 10)

"Roses of Picardy": Popular song of World War I, it inspires the name of Morag's imaginary childhood companion, Rosa Picardy. (pp. 10-11)

alter ego: One's other self. (p. 13)

infantile paralysis: Polio. (p. 16)

South Wachakwa: Small Manitoba town near Manawaka. (p. 18)

PART II • CHAPTER 2

Summary

Another mid-June morning: Morag is awakened by a phone call. The early caller turns out to be a would-be writer seeking advice on how to get published. Morag handles the call politely and with suppressed exasperation. The essence of her advice is that you just have to work like hell. When the caller, offended, slams down the phone, Morag feels typically guilty.

Morag muses, gazing out over the river, which, caught by the morning sun, looks like liquid bronze. Her thoughts are interrupted by the arrival of Royland, who has brought her a fresh fish for breakfast. Royland reveals that he is going divining on Friday morning. He wonders if Morag would like to accompany him. Morag eagerly responds.

When Royland asks why she is so interested in divining, Morag hesitates. Then she admits that she finds it hard to believe in and yet she believes in it totally. Royland says simply: "It works." He does not need to understand it, he says; he just has to do it. When Royland leaves, Morag wraps the fish in aluminium foil and puts it in the refrigerator. She looks at her snapshots and then into her mirror. As she studies her reflection, the films in her head start up again. How true they are, how often they have been refilmed, how much they have been edited, she does not know.

She can smell the prairie dust on Hill Street outside Christie Logan's house. The comfortably-off lived in the big brick houses on the hilltop. Christie's house was typical of the poor section of the prairie town, a square two-storey wooden box whose brown paint had long since gone, the yard a junk-pile.

Memorybank Movie #2 begins on this note: the smell of urine in Christie's house is the first thing Morag is struck by.

A Big Fat Woman is telling her that she'll like living in town when she gets used to it. A Skinny Man tells her that he is Christie and his wife is Prin. Prin takes Morag up to her new room.

The next year is a blank in Morag's mind. Memorybank Movie #3 picks up when she is six and Christie is leading her to school for the first time. She is afraid and doesn't want to go. Christie tells her she'll have no trouble if she gives them hell. He tries to suggest that all people are the same, but she doesn't understand.

When the children start laughing at her and commenting on her long dress, she doesn't know what's wrong. Then she notices all of the girls' dresses are short, bright and new. Then she sees Eva Winkler, the girl next door, dressed like her. She is momentarily reassured, until she notices that Eva is crying.

Morag's first day of school is a confusion of details, fears, insecurities, words and concepts she doesn't understand. She soon realizes that she can't see the blackboard properly, but she can hear all that's going on. And some of that is not pleasant. The name-calling and mocking of Eva after she has soiled her pants strikes Morag hard. At the end of the first day she is disillusioned about school.

Memorybank Movie #4 stars the much older Morag. Now she is seven and can read. She is quiet, stubborn and defiant.

When Morag comes home from school, Prin is usually eating jelly doughnuts. Prin is not very bright. When she tells Morag stories about her background, Morag is aware of Prin's grammatical errors. She informs Morag that she married Christie when he came back from the Great War (World War I) and that her real name is Princess. Morag finds this last piece of information wildly inappropriate.

Christie is a short, skinny, strong man. His face is usually unshaven, his teeth are bad and his overalls are always baggy. But the worst thing is that he always stinks. He is the town garbageman. One day he takes Morag on his horse-drawn wagon to the garbage dump, called the Nuisance Grounds. She doesn't know why the place is referred to as the "Nuisance Grounds," nor does she know why Christie is called a Scavenger, but she is afraid to ask.

When some of her fellow-pupils start loudly taunting Christie and her, Morag is mortified. But Christie plays along with them, acting like a fool. After the kids leave, Morag begins to cry. She asks Christie why he had to act so silly. Christie replies that he was just giving them what they wanted. Then he starts to philosophize: "By their garbage shall ye know them," Christie declares. He tells Morag that he sees what people throw out, and from this evidence he learns about their secret lives. He doesn't care, but he says they think he does, and therefore cannot meet him face-to-face. "They think muck's dirty. It's no more dirty than what's in their heads."

Memorybank Movie #5 is set in the heat of August. Morag is fascinated by the swarms of bluebottle flies in the smelly, dirty, run-down house. How can they be beautiful and dirty at the same time? Prin doesn't bother to keep the house clean. Most of the time she just sits. It is Morag's job to go to Parson's Bakery to buy jelly doughnuts. Once, while waiting, Morag hears Mrs. McVitie and Mrs. Cameron making loud comments about people who can afford jelly doughnuts and about

Morag's scruffy appearance. Morag sticks out her tongue at them at runs home. She tells Prin she'll never go into that bakery again, and, when Prin asks why, Morag tells her exactly what she heard.

Prin is upset. She apologizes to Morag for not looking after her better and explains how she long ago let things go with her appearance and the house. She reveals her lack of understanding of Christie and why he married her.

That evening, the three of them are sitting on the front porch. Their neighbour, Gus Winkler, starts yelling at his runny-nosed son, Vernon. Then he starts beating Vernon with a stick. Morag, horrified sees blood on Vernon's face. Christie just sits there, doing nothing, but after the two Winklers go back into their house, he castigates himself for his inaction. Prin says it wasn't any of his business, but Christie gets up and walks into the house. Prin says he is going to have "one of his spells."

When Morag and Prin re-enter the house, Christie is sitting and shaking. His eyes are blank. After a long time he stops shaking, but keeps sitting, motionless. Prin quietly explains that Christie suffers from shell-shock from the War. It comes and goes; nothing can be done about it. The shell-shock is the reason he could get no better job than Scavenger, Prin says. That night, in her room, Morag thinks that while Christie may smell and look dumb, he wouldn't ever beat her.

Memorybank Movie #6: "Christie with Spirits" presents Morag in a supporting role to the undoubted star, Christie Logan. In this movie, Morag is nine and it is winter. Inside the Logan kitchen it is warm and Christie is warmer, being well-fortified with red biddy, a mixture of cheap red wine and methylated spirits. Prin is annoyed by Christie's drinking, so he starts talking to Morag.

Fired by the alcohol, Christie launches into a long tirade and lament. All the fine families of the town — the Connors, the McVities, the Pearls and the Camerons — may look down on him, but the Logan clan is as good as any of theirs.

Combining assertions, rhetorical questions and exclamations, Christie describes his ancestry. His clan is an ancient clan; his people are an ancient people. "This is the Valour of My Ancestors" is his motto; "The Ridge of Tears" is his war-cry. He repeats the latter in Gaelic, although he is unsure of the pronunciation. He goes on about the Sassenach (English) soldiers who massacred the Highland Scots at Culloden in 1746.

He drags out his copy of *The Clans and Tartans of Scotland* and asks Morag to describe the crest of the Logans. She knows it off by heart: "A passion nail piercing a human heart, proper." Christie is pleased, but then gets gloomy. "Och, what the hell does it matter? It's here we live, not there, and the glory has passed away, and likely never was in the first place." Morag interrupts to ask him to tell her the story of Piper Gunn, her legendary ancestor.

Christie's First Tale of Piper Gunn begins. In the Northern Scottish Highlands of Sutherland, a long time ago, the Bitch-Duchess, a dark, cold-hearted woman, was turning people out of their homes. People who had farmed for centuries were dispossessed of their lands and driven to the seashore, to live upon the rocks. The Bitch-Duchess was thinking only of how the lands could be used for sheep-raising and making money.

Piper Gunn was amongst those scraping for a living by the sea. Piper was of the Clan Gunn. A tall man whose voice was like a drum, whose heart was that of a child, whose courage was that of a thousand men, he had the strength of conviction — faith. So he played his pipes, and his laments roused the people to a sense of what they had lost.

Piper told the people to board a ship which would be arriving the next morning. "Let us go to the New World," he said. They were doubtful and afraid, so Piper Gunn cursed them and said he and his wife, who was named Morag, would go. The others could rot. Then he changed his tune, and his bagpipes played battle music, march after march, concluding with "The Gunn's Salute."

When the ship arrived in the morning, Morag, her child and her husband marched onto the ship. Inspired by their example, and fired by the music of the bagpipes, all of the others followed them onto the ship and left for the New World. They ended up at the Red River.

Morag goes to bed. She thinks of her notebook in her top dresser drawer. She will never show her scribbler to anyone; she will write in it tomorrow. She begins to make up a story: "Morag's Tale of Piper Gunn's Women."

Commentary

The chapter opens in the present in Morag's house on the

river. As in all chapters but the last, a present consideration unreels the memorybank movies which then unfold chronologically. This structure helps reinforce one of the key themes of the novel — the presence of the past. We evolve from the earlier stages of our life history; what we *were* is part of who we *are*.

Morag's reflections on the river and on how one can catch the truth of it in words is typical of her. At the end of the chapter the nine-year-old Morag is musing on the meaning of "mooner." She knows what it means: someone who moons about, dawdling and thinking — like Morag. But to her it means something else — "some . . . creature from another planet. Left here accidentally." A few minutes later she is wondering "What means *The Strength of Conviction*?" This fascination with words — with meanings, truth and invention, fact and fiction — stays with her throughout her life. Already she is composing stories about the ancestral (probably mythical) Morag Gunn. History and fiction intertwine.

Early in the chapter we meet Morag's neighbour, old Royland. He divines for water. When Morag tells Royland that she finds divining both hard to believe in and something she believes in totally, the paradox is not surprising. His observation that one does not need to understand the process of divining is not lost on Morag. One just has to do it, he says. He has the strength of conviction that she so admires in Christie's tales of Piper and Morag Gunn. *He* has faith. *She* must have faith if she is to write. But still she wonders: *how* can one make words do the magic?

In her memorybank movies of her Manawaka past, we meet Morag's first diviner, Christie. A man with little formal education, Christie is her first true teacher. He shows her how to look below the surface and divine what truths, meanings and significance there may be in what most people overlook or discard as unimportant.

As a child, living with the town garbageman and being poor, Morag knows what it is to feel an outsider. She determines on her first day in school that she will never let people know when she is afraid. She will not let them get to her, even though their taunts of Christie and her old dresses humiliate her.

Paradoxically, to be a writer, Morag must reveal herself and her vulnerabilities in her fiction. Fiction provides a means to be oneself, to be free: in fiction, although one wears masks and disguises, reality is created through which essential truths can be revealed.

Christie's philosophy of garbage influences Morag in at least two other ways. What he recovers from what other people throw away reveals their history, just as what he absorbs from what he has read, heard, and lived through reveals the interlocking of the histories, myths and fictions of his people. Nothing is ever truly thrown away. The writer, Morag soon appreciates, is a scavenger — just like Christie.

Similarly, Christie's philosophy of the "socialism of the junk heap" is significant. Garbage is communal property, he tells Morag. One must share. One is an individual *and* a member of the human community. This lesson will not be lost on Morag.

It is Christie's telling stories to young Morag which first fires her desire to be a writer. Entranced by his tales, Morag starts creating her own tales, her own created realities.

Notes

Freudian error (Freudian slip): Named after Sigmund Freud, father of modern Psychoanalysis. In psychoanalytic theory, this involves a temporary breakdown of a person's normal defenses. What is going on in the person's unconscious mind (often of a sexual nature) then slips out. (p. 24)

ambiguity: Something capable of being interpreted many different ways. Ambiguous: Indefinite; open to different interpretations. (p. 25)

divining: The art of discovering underground sources of water; the finding of something hidden; knowing intuitively. The word is associated with the divine, the holy, the god-like. Water-dowsing is the technical name for the kind of divining Royland does. (p. 26)

The Great War: World War I, supposedly the war to end all wars. (p. 34)

Gaelic: The language spoken by the descendents of the Gaels, an ancient people who settled in Ireland and Scotland. (p. 42)

shell-shock: A neurosis originating in being under fire in modern warfare. (p. 45)

relief: Government assistance given out to the unemployed of

Canada during the Great Depression of the 1930s. (p. 46)

clan: A subdivision of a tribe, it is made up of families sharing a common ancestor — especially in the Scottish Highlands. (p. 47)

Culloden: Scene of the breaking up of the Scottish clans by the English in 1746. It has become the symbol of the brutal suppression of Scotland by the English colonialists. (p. 47)

Sassenach: Gaelic word for Englishman. (p. 47)

Charlie: Bonnie Prince Charlie, Roman Catholic pretender to the Scottish throne in the mid-eighteenth century after the 1707 Union of Scotland and England. (p. 48)

pibroch: Musical variations on a lament or martial theme played on the bagpipes. (p. 50)

Red River: This river in southern Manitoba, which flows north into Lake Winnipeg, gave its name to the Red River Settlements. Here Métis and Scottish settlers established what was to become the Province of Manitoba. (p. 51)

CHAPTER 3

Summary

Morag begins her day as usual but hopes this morning will be better: she hopes to hear from Pique.

A-Okay, Maudie, and young Tom Smith drop by to see her. A-Okay, whose real name is Alf, has brought Morag some of his poems. He is a tall, awkward man in his late twenties who is always bumping into or breaking things. Like Morag, he is short-sighted; however, he seldom wears his glasses. A good man, he acts as Morag's "unofficial protector." Maudie is also in her late twenties and is what was called in the sixties an "earth mother." Her hand-sewn dress and long, natural blonde hair go with her plain, clean face.

Tom, at eight, has been reading for three years and is ostracized by children his age for being not only bright but encyclopedic in his knowledge. Even Morag feels a bit intimidated by him. His parents are determined to treat him as an equal, hoping to avoid his being alienated from them when he comes into his teens. Morag reflects that she had once felt that way herself. Now she thinks that most of the crises that happens to others eventually happen to you.

Maudie says that Pique must have been compelled to go

out west and that she has a right not to contact her mother. Morag is annoyed, but tries not to show it. Sending one post-card would not spoil Pique's process of self-discovery, she says. She is unconvinced by Maudie's statement that, symbolically, it might. Then Morag feels guilty when "back-to-the-land" Maudie and A-Okay offer to start digging up her garden for planting. Morag has no time to garden; she must work at her writing to support herself. A-Okay agrees that writing is Morag's real work; it is there she has to make her statement. Morag says nothing, but thinks that, for her, writing is not making statements about life. Writing is giving life to people who breathe and move within her head and who must be given a voice.

At this moment, the phone rings. It is Pique's father, whom Morag has not heard from in three years. Pique had turned up at his place in Toronto, and he demands to know why Morag allowed her to leave home. Morag blasts him in return, but they eventually agree that neither is to blame for Pique's departure. After a few awkward words, they hang up.

Morag sits silent and motionless. Then she tells the Smiths that it was Pique's father on the phone. Guiltily, she adds that since she herself never had an ever-present father, she has denied one to her daughter. Maudie and A-Okay sense that it is time to leave. After they are gone, Morag reflects on her own past and her changing interpretations of it. These reflections lead into Memorybank Movie #7.

Twelve-year-old Morag has come into puberty and feels herself to be a woman. She is also a tomboy. Her toughness makes her feel contempt for her best friend Eva Winkler, who is still beaten by her father. Eva is "gutless," and Morag vows she'll never be like that.

One day, Morag overhears some of the teachers gossiping about her. One finds her difficult; another thinks she's perhaps "not quite all there." Miss McMurtrie thinks Morag is bright, but that she doesn't seem to care. Mr. Tate blames the home environment. Morag eavesdrops, but never lets on what she has overheard.

On another occasion, Morag is copying out a poem for school. Christie sees the poem ("Daffodils" by William Words-worth) and dismisses it as nonsense. He says he will read her a *real* poem. The English call it a forgery, but Ossian's epic about the Gaelic hero, Cuchullin, is what fires Christie's imagination. Morag is similarly sparked, and they both wish they could understand the Gaelic in which the poem was originally written.

In the classroom, Morag is afraid to admit that she cannot see the blackboard properly. She still believes it dangerous to reveal her vulnerabilities. Morag's pride also shows in her singing out loud in class, in her chopping her old dresses shorter than anyone else's, in her forthright answer to the teacher who catches her daydreaming. One day, after refusing to show her hurt pride over misspelling a word in class, she catches the eye of Jules "Skinner" Tonnerre, a member of the local Métis (half French, half Indian) family shunned by the "nice" people of Manawaka. His grin makes her feel akin to him in his contempt for the others. She grins back. Morag starts thinking about boys — and Skinner in particular. His vulgarity is never directed at her. She wonders if it is because he respects her or if it is because he doesn't consider her pretty enough to be worth embarrassing.

At the end of the day, when the class is patriotically singing "The Maple Leaf Forever" Morag realizes that the symbols of the thistle, rose, shamrock and maple leaf have no meaning for Jules. She looks in his direction and notices that he is not singing.

Memorybank Movie #8 deals with Christie's gift of the garbage-telling.

Morag goes alone to the Nuisance Grounds just to see what the place is like. The dump, which is on the same hill as the cemetery where Morag's parents are buried, is screened from public view by clusters of chokecherry and pineberry bushes. Morag is particularly struck by the stench and the swarms of flies.

Suddenly, she sees Skinner there, holding a bent crowbar and a pair of pliers. She is frightened but tries not to show it. Instead, she acts aggressively. When Skinner makes an obscene comment about her, Morag starts bragging about her ancestors. Then Skinner begins to speak about his ancestors and the North-West Rebellion of 1885. Morag has never heard of this part of Canadian history and wants to hear more.

Just then, Christie arrives on his garbage wagon. He is surprised to see Morag there with Skinner. As he shovels the garbage off the wagon, he asks if he had ever explained how to "tell" the garbage the way that some tell fortunes. Skinner snorts with laughter and Morag feels ashamed of Christie, but the two young people stay to listen.

Christie maintains that he can tell a great deal about the town's people just by looking at what they discard. Some steak bones reveal that Simon Pearl, the lawyer, is eating steak once a week, although he pretends to be poor. A pile of apple peels reveals that the Reverend McKee received a crate of apples from his sister in the Okanagan, but the peels obviously have not been used for compost in his garden. Paint tins from the Connors' show that Grandfather Connor is on a painting rampage to make the others in his family feel lazy.

Slowly, suspensefully, Christie builds up to his revelation to Morag and Skinner that he had once found a dead newborn baby wrapped in newspapers. He buried it in the Nuisance Grounds because it was a nuisance to the mother, who had put it in the garbage can. He won't reveal who did it, but he knows. When Morag presses him to reveal the identity of the mother, he says it would do no good and that it's none of her business. He keeps his secret, but he feels it was a terrible thing to have witnessed.

Memorybank Movie #9 stars Morag in Sunday School. Morag decides to show Mrs. McKee, the minister's wife, a poem she has written. Mrs. McKee shows surprise that Morag writes poetry and says it is just fine. Then she comments that a poem about the Three Wise Men would be set in the desert and that Morag's phrase about "wintry blast" would not be appropriate. Morag blushes with shame, then makes several attempts to revise the poem. When she gets something more satisfactory, she shows the revision to Mrs. McKee, who offhandedly approves and then tells her to sit down. Others in the class start making fun of Morag.

After auditions for the carol solo for Christmas Eve, Mrs. McKee announces that she will read the class a poem. Morag assumes that it is her poem, and imagines the effect it will have on her classmates. The poem turns out to be one by Hilaire Belloc. It, too, is a Christmas poem. When Morag hears it, she wonders how anyone could write something that good. At home, she burns her own poem in the stove.

The next Sunday, Morag finds out that Vanessa MacLeod has been chosen to sing the Christmas solo. Morag complains to

Christie that it's not fair, and Christie replies that life isn't fair. Morag admits that Vanessa's voice is not bad, but when Vanessa sings, Morag silently finds fault with the silly lyrics and hopes something awful will happen to her.

A month later, Morag hears that Vanessa's father, Dr. MacLeod, is dead. Christie calls him a fine man; and Morag feels guilty for having wished ill on Vanessa. Vanessa returns to school and Morag cannot bring herself to speak to her. Morag sees that Vanessa is more reserved than ever.

Memorybank Movie #10 holds a story within a story. Christie is drinking while Morag does her homework. Christie asks Morag is she wants to hear more about Piper Gunn, and Morag, pleased, closes her geography book.

Christie's "Tale of Piper Gunn and the Long March" is told in the vivid, rhetorical epic style of the born storyteller. Christie picks up the story of Piper and Morag Gunn and the Sutherlanders being landed at the wrong place on Hudson Bay. The story relates the hardship and suffering — the battle for survival — experienced on the long journey to the Red River Country, near Manawaka, where they settle.

Afterwards, Morag goes to bed but not to sleep. She writes in her scribbler — which is now almost filled — about Morag Gunn, her namesake, and how she built an elaborately carved chariot in the wilds of Manitoba for her people. She is also working on another story about Clowny MacPherson, a scrawny little woodcutter who is laughed at because he looks silly. Piper Gunn, however, respects him. Morag falls asleep with the determination to write more the next day.

Memorybank Movie #11 begins with Christie searching for something and getting into an argument with Prin. The fight becomes bitter and Morag, who is listening, becomes confused as they bicker about their own failures.

Christie finds his faded copy of *The 60th Canadian Field Artillery Battery Book* from World War I. It is the history of the regiment he and Morag's father served in from 1916 to 1919. One of the pictures of the battery shows Colin Gunn and Christie, but Christie cannot distinguish one man from another. Morag is disappointed. Christie reveals that her father saved his life in the Battle of Bourlon Wood. Together Morag and Christie read through the dry, academic account of the battle given in the book. Christie maintains that the book makes the war sound like a Sunday school picnic. He tells the story his way, depicting the horrors of the death-filled, muddy trenches. At one point, a man next to Christie was blown to bits. Christie thought it was Colin, and passed out. . . .

Christie stops the story suddenly. He is shaking. He says he regrets finding the book and goes to bed. When Morag asks Prin if she can have the book, Prin says that Christie would not give it up. Christie has overheard the request, however. The next morning, although he refuses to part with the book, he gives Morag a knife. It is about eight inches long, with a dark brown leathery handle on which is carved a horizontal "T." Christie does not know what the symbol stands for.

But he tells Morag how he got the knife: it had been traded to Christie years ago by a youth for a pack of cigarettes. Later, the youth was killed when he ploughed his truck head on into a freight train. Christie has never given Morag a present before, except for candies. Morag is ashamed of the present and feels bad about being ashamed. She shoves the knife into the back of her drawer.

Commentary

In this chapter, we are introduced to Pique's father. However, we do not learn until later in Part 3 that Pique's father and the character Jules Tonnerre (Skinner) are actually the same person.

When we first meet Jules, he is a 15-year-old Métis schoolboy in Manawaka. He and Morag are classmates, and Morag feels somehow that he is a kindred spirit.

One day the class is singing "The Maple Leaf Forever." Morag notices that Jules is not participating. His people, part French, part Indian, are not in the song. Morag stops singing, without knowing quite why. It is the beginning of her long identification with Jules — as a person, as a representative of the Métis and, like herself, as an outsider.

Jules is another one of the diviners in Morag's life. He, too, has a concern for the past of his people. Soon Morag is listening to stories that have been passed down to Jules from his father, stories of the prairies from a Métis point-of-view. These stories differ radically from the stories she has heard from Christie or learned from Canadian history books, because they are told from an entirely different perspective. Morag notes this. What

33

we choose to recall or emphasize about the past is what we see (or want to see) as significant. Christie tells young Morag "We believe what we know." And Morag later acknowledges that there is "no one version" of the truth.

This distinction also comes through when Christie drags out the official history of his World War I regiment. The dry, cold, matter-of-factness of the account makes the Battle of Bourlon Wood sound to Christie "like a Sunday school picnic." His account, on the other hand, emphasizes the mud, the cold and the terror of the battle of which he and Morag's father were actually a part. His personal account is much more human, much more alive, and much more *present* than the facts the official story recounts.

It is worth commenting further on the stories of Jules and of Christie, for they foreshadow Morag's concerns as a writer. "The Maple Leaf Forever," for example, is a song celebrating the British conquest of Canada and referring to the settlers from England, Ireland and Scotland. The poem "Daffodils" — which Morag studies in school — is likewise a colonial poem, imported from outside. The stories of Jules and Christie, however, are authentic growths from the native Canadian soil of the prairies. Similarly, Morag's books will grow out of Manitoba, out of her roots in Manawaka.

The introduction in this chapter of the hunting knife with a "T" symbol burned into its handle seems insignificant at this point. On the very last page of Chapter 3, Christie gives young Morag this knife and tells how he came by it. Later, in Chapter 10, we will discover one of the mysterious roles this knife plays.

Notes

Susanna Moodie: Genteel English settler in the Peterborough (Ontario) region in the 1830s, she was the sister of Catharine Parr Traill. She is most famous for her classic journal of pioneer life, *Roughing It in the Bush* (1852). (p. 57)

"The Thistle Shamrock Rose Entwine the Maple Leaf Forever": The symbols of Scotland, Ireland, England, and Canada. This is the last line of the English-Canadian patriotic song, "The Maple Leaf Forever" by Alexander Muir (1867). The song ignored French-Canadians, Native Peoples, and all the non-British elements in Canada. (p. 61)

William Wordsworth: English Romantic poet (1770-1850). His poem "Daffodils" begins with the line "I wandered lonely as a cloud" and was, for years, a favourite selection for memory work in schools. (p. 63)

Cuchullin: Legendary Gaelic hero. (p. 63)

Ossian (Oisin): Supposedly a Gaelic hero and poet of the third century A.D., most scholars believe he was the invention of James Macpherson, whose "translations" of the poems of Ossian in the 1760s became both popular and influential. (p. 64)

Cloud Cuckoo Land: Dreamland. (p. 68)

breeds, half-breeds: The Métis people, descendents of native people and early French-Canadian fur traders. The Tonnerre family are Métis. (p. 69)

donkless: Mispronunciation of *dauntless* (fearless). (p. 69).

Wolfe: James Wolfe (1727-1759). British commander of the victorious troops in the Battle of the Plains of Abraham. He and the French commander, Montcalm, died after the battle on September 13, 1759, which assured the British conquest of New France and the establishment of what became Canada. (p. 69)

Tabernac: Perhaps the most famous of French-Canadian swearwords, it is considered a blasphemy against the Roman Catholic Church. (p. 72)

The Troubles: Euphemism for the North-West Rebellion of 1885 which resulted in the suppression of the Métis by the English-Canadian authorities. (p. 73)

"Oh what a piece of work is man.": Line from William Shakespeare's *Hamlet*. Hamlet's speech deals with the seemingly contradictory nature of man. It is thus appropriate here. (p. 88)

Amiens, Arras, Cambrai, Valenciennes, Mons, Bourlon Wood: Scenes of battles in France and Belgium during World War I in which Canadian troops were involved. (pp. 89-90)

CHAPTER 4

Summary

Morag is awakened by the birds on the roof of her log house. As she gets up to prepare for going divining with Royland, she imagines the struggles for survival of pioneers such as the Coopers, who originally built the log house she now owns. Was life better or worse in those days? Morag doubts that the pioneers worried about their daughters, as she does about Pique. Nor were they impelled, as she is, to work out their inner struggles on paper. Suddenly the character Catharine Parr Traill comes to mind. Mrs. Traill was a formidable pioneer who lived in the area over 100 years ago. She was a wife and mother, a writer, and an amateur botanist who knew how to use her environment to provide for her family. Mrs. Traill's practical imagination seemed inexhaustible: she taught herself how to start an orchard, how to make a thousand useful things from the birch tree, and how to make wholesome menus from scratch. Morag feels decidedly inferior as a new pioneer in an old log house complete with all the modern conveniences.

As she sits musing over her fourth cup of coffee, Morag's fertile imagination conjures up a scene at the Traill Homestead, circa 1840. Unlike Morag, Mrs. Traill would be fully awake when she got up and would accomplish a multitude of tasks "all before lunch." In an imaginary dialogue with Catharine Parr Traill, Morag reflects that the disappearance of Pique is a minor emergency compared to the life-threatening situations faced by the pioneers.

This dialogue is interrupted by Royland's knock on the door. The conversation then turns to Pique, and Morag's mixed emotions emerge. She realizes her daughter needs to be on her own, but she is worried: the previous year, Pique had landed in a mental hospital in Toronto after taking LSD. This painful memory sets off self-recriminations in Morag. A montage of memories floods her mind: Pique in the mental hospital, denying that Morag is her mother; Pique at five, asking her mother to tell her a story about a robin; Pique in England, asking if they are going home and Morag not knowing where home is; two visits by Pique's father, ten years apart. Pique rejecting her, despising her. . . . Royland assures Morag that Pique does not despise her. Rather, she has mixed feelings, as Morag does.

After coffee at the Smith's farm, Morag and Royland go outside. Royland grasps his Y-shaped divining rod and starts to walk back and forth. At first the rod does not twitch and A-Okay is doubtful that the method works. Even when young Tom, silenced by the mystery of divining, suddenly shouts that the wand *is* twitching, A-Okay is skeptical. As it turns out, the driller *does* find water — precisely where Royland's magic wand had pointed. When A-Okay observes that he doesn't understand how it's done, Royland agrees. He doesn't either; he just knows it happens.

That night Pique telephones from Winnipeg to say that she is fine. Her friend Gord is with her. She relates some of the highlights of her travels: she visited Manawaka; her guitar almost got broken; and she almost got charged by the police after a run-in with some drunks outside a small town in Manitoba. Her arm, which was cut in that incident (a drunk threw a broken beer bottle at her), is okay.

The last words of mother and daughter to each other are the familiar expressions of "take care." Pique hangs up, and silence echoes in the house. Morag goes out to look at the river, dark and shining in the moonlight. She feels an unreasonable and incredible "lightening of the heart."

Memorybank Movie #12 unrolls. Morag, now in her early teens, is in church with Prin, who increasingly embarrasses her. Morag has become fashion-conscious. She works in Simlow's Ladies' Wear on Saturdays and spends all her money on clothes. Her efforts to get Prin to dress nicely and do her hair up in a bun seem doomed to failure. Morag feels guilty for her shame, but back home she announces that she won't go to church again.

Memorybank Movie #13 takes place in the store where Morag works part-time with Millie Cristopherson on Saturdays. There, under Millie's tutelage, Morag is learning about "Good Taste" as defined by Millie. She observes, condescendingly, the "Awful Taste" of the snobbish townswomen, and notes the poor farmers' wives who are always just looking. When Eva Winkler comes in, poorly dressed, pale hair straggling, the runny-nosed Vern in tow, Morag makes excuses not to have to talk with her — even though Eva was once her best friend.

After work, Morag goes to the Parthenon Café, where Julie Kazlik works. They eventually end up sitting with two boys in a car, watching the Saturday night activities on Main Street.

Parking on Main Street is one of the great excitements of life in the small town. Lots of people are out — farmers in their good suits; wives all dressed up; town whores scouting for business, some of them already with soldiers from the nearby military base. And then, to Morag's dismay, there is Christie sauntering down the street. Morag is mortified when he puts on his "doormat act" and plays the simpleton in front of two of the town's lawyers. The awkward silence in the car is broken by Morag's observation that Ina Spettigue is with *three* soldiers. An older boy arrives to reclaim the car, and the big Saturday Night on the Town comes to an end.

Memorybank Movie #14 is set in Morag's Grade Nine English class at Manawaka Collegiate. Morag worships her teacher, Miss Melrose. The latter encourages Morag in her writing and also convinces Morag that she needs glasses.

In Memorybank Movie #15, Morag has a brief encounter with Skinner Tonnerre down in the valley of the Wachakwa Creek. That evening, Christie tells Morag the tale of Piper Gunn and the Rebels. Morag likes the story, even though Christie's version does not quite conform with Morag's knowledge of Canadian History and the Riel Rebellion.

Memorybank Movie #16 is called, dramatically, "Down in the Valley, Act II." Morag, now in Grade 11, meets Jules, who is on leave from the army. They have hardly spoken since the earlier, brief encounter in the valley. Over coffee in the Parthenon Café, Jules tells Morag about his family. He takes her to the collection of shacks he calls home. They make love, and Jules then introduces Morag to his father, Lazarus. Lazarus is bitter and defiant. He is only 39, but has lived a hard life and looks much older. Jules returns to camp and Morag thinks about him in the days that follow. She reads in the *Winnipeg Free Press* about the disastrous Dieppe Raid and anxiously scans the casualty lists in the paper. The name of Jules Tonnerre does not appear. At night, as Morag lies awake thinking of Jules, some of the stories he told her about his Métis past flash into her head — tales of his ancestor, Chevalier (Rider) Tonnerre as a young man roaming the plains and, as an old man — a follower of Louis Riel. Interestingly, Jules' version of the "true story" is different from both Christie's version and the official, "historical" version.

Memorybank Movie #17: The dancehall at the RCAF training base at South Wachakwa is named "The Flamingo." Morag sometimes goes here on a Saturday night. Whereas she finds the men dull and chauvinistic, Eva — who is blonde and submissive — is popular at the dances. Then Eva discovers that she is pregnant. Terrified of her father's reaction, she aborts herself with a clotheshanger. The bleeding is severe, and Eva is rushed to the hospital, where an operation is performed that will leave her sterile. Her father, Gus, is not told the truth. He believes that his daughter was anaemic and haemorrhaging. As for the aborted baby, Morag realizes that it will be buried in the Nuisance Grounds — the town's unofficial cemetery. Now Morag is even more determined that absolutely nothing will stop her from getting out of Manawaka.

Memorybank Movie #18, "The Banner," co-stars Morag Gunn, cub reporter, and Lachlan MacLachlan, eccentric editor of *The Manawaka Banner*. After the death of his son at Dieppe, Lachlan takes to drinking and is frequently hungover. Morag is the staff writer and is learning how to proofread and do layouts. She wants to rewrite the Local Reports in proper newspaper style, but Lachlan refuses to allow this, cautioning her against pretension. People want to read them as they are, he says: *The Banner* is a small-town paper. She must not look down on people just because she has a knack with words.

Ladies from Winnipeg's Junior League bring a collection of prints of paintings to Manawaka. Morag covers the show (only three people attend the opening) for *The Banner*. She is very moved by one particular picture of a beautiful girl. Back in the office, she writes up her report four times. Lachlan checks her article and then points out that Morag has made a naïve mistake. The painting that so impressed her was not recently painted in Winnipeg, as she had thought. Rather, it is part of a larger painting, *Venus Rising From the Waves*, by the Italian Renaissance painter, Sandro Botticelli.

Humiliated by her ignorance, Morag crumples up her report. Lachlan rebukes her for her pride, saying that an admission of ignorance is neither shameful nor uncommon. Morag disagrees, but when Lachlan brings in a book on art, she spends a long time looking at it.

Memorybank Movie #19: "Down in the Valley, Act III" is set on a winter night. Lachlan instructs Morag to report on a fire down in the valley at the Tonnerre shacks. The eldest girl and her children have been "caught in it." Morag balks, but then reluctantly trudges through the snow to the valley, thinking back to what she remembers about Piquette Tonnerre and her painful life.

The shacks are in ruins. The policeman, a doctor and the

undertaker are there. Lazarus also stands by, but it is too late. Morag is terribly shaken and vomits in the snow. When she gets back to the office, Lachlan pours her a shot of rye and apologizes for sending her. He had not realized it would be so bad.

Memorybank Movie #20 is the last one in Part Two of *The Diviners*.

The War is over. Morag's earnings as a reporter have been added to her trust fund monies, enabling her to go to college in Winnipeg in the fall of 1945. Her feelings about finally leaving Manawaka are a mixture of joy and guilt.

Prin has become a vegetable and Christie will have to look after her now. Although he seldom gets drunk, he is scrawnier than ever, and dirty and smelly. He repulses Morag, who thinks he purposely brings on his strange fits. He bewails his wasted life and raves on about his ancestors, whom he feels he has disgraced. Morag escapes Christie's interminable ramblings and silences by going out. One evening she runs into Jules, dressed in casual civilian clothes. After a grin, he begins an awkward conversation. Morag asks after Lazarus, and Jules says things are not well with him. Then he mentions the fire. He knows Morag covered the story and asks her if she saw his sister. "No," she says. When Morag speaks of going to college in Winnipeg and never coming back, Jules mocks her. Morag will succeed in life. She'll marry a rich professor, he says. He doesn't know what he's going to do, and claims he doesn't care. "I don't have to *do* anything all that much. I'm not like you." Morag realizes the truth of it. They live in different worlds now. When Jules leaves her with a "See you around, eh?" he does not look back.

Commentary

Whereas Chapter 3 ended with the young Morag inheriting (unknowingly) the Tonnerre knife, Chapter 4 begins with the middle-aged Morag inheriting (knowingly) the old Cooper house she has bought on the river near McConnell's Landing. The young Morag was ashamed of Christie's present of the knife. She hid it in a drawer, seeking to deny it. Now she is filling the pioneers' old house with second-hand Ontario furniture from the nineteenth century, proud of establishing her links with the past she once sought to reject: "The oldness of the farmhouse, the roughness, were qualities Morag would have loathed as a kid.

Now she valued them." Thus we can see an evolution in Morag: foolish pride has been replaced by genuine pride; the past has found its place in her present. A survivor herself, she is following consciously in the footsteps of her adopted ancestors.

The introduction of another spiritual forebear, the Peterborough pioneer Catharine Parr Traill, also figures largely in this chapter. Morag conjures her up and makes her into a mentor and a measuring stick, an inspiration and an admonition. She is also making a connection with local history. Later, as Morag becomes more self-assured, she is able to dismiss Catharine Parr Traill and finally become her own person.

Another link in Morag's awareness of time is evident in this chapter. She realizes that the world she inherited is not the same as the one her daughter has inherited. Pique's story of a bad experience while hitch-hiking in Manitoba makes Morag compare the difficulties of her past with the hazards of her daughter's world: "My world in those days was a residual bad dream . . . with some goodness and some chance of climbing out. Hers is an accomplished nightmare, with nowhere to go. . . ."

As a teenager, Morag's gradual understanding of the Métis parallels her growing relationship with Jules Tonnerre. From him, she learns his people's version of "the Canadian story." Meeting his father, Lazarus, seeing the ramshackle homes the Tonnerres live in, hearing the legends that have been handed down to Jules — all these factors make her more conscious of how life is always different for others. She becomes increasingly concerned with the validity of so-called "facts." "What is a true story? Is there any such thing?" These questions bother Morag. She believes the only certainty is the deadness of the dead. (Contrast this with her later realization that Christie, Lazarus and Catharine Parr Traill have not died, but live on in the human imagination through poem and song, story and myth-making).

The theme of writing as being both work *and* a gift ties in with two central preoccupations of the novel. The Protestant work ethic — so strong a theme in Canadian Literature — is evident here: one must work in order to justify oneself. The idea of writing as a gift may relate to the parable of Jesus about the talents (see Matthew 25: 14-30, where we are told that the "unprofitable servant" who does not put his talents to work, will be thrown into "outer darkness"). Thus Morag feels she *must* write.

Finally, the pictures given in this chapter of small-town life on the Prairies are worth attention. A close observer, Morag becomes aware of the class divisions in Manawaka: for example, Christie Logan is never addressed as Mr. Logan; but Simon Pearl and Archie McVitie, lawyers, are always referred to as Mr. Pearl and Mr. McVitie. Morag finds the confining nature of small-town life increasingly horrific.

If "Gainsay (deny) Who Dare" is the war-cry she later adopts, we see her in this chapter as a teenager trying to deny herself and her background. Ashamed of her poverty, of Prin and Christie and her friend Eva — all of which she feels guilty about — she tries bravely to fit in with the crowd. This need for approval and acceptance by one's desired peers is typically adolescent. In seeking to be tactful, well-dressed and popular (trying to be who she is not) Morag is laying the framework for her eventual marriage. In trying to deny her true self and to start fresh, she is taking a false turn in her life.

It is with mixed feelings of joy and guilt that she leaves the prairie town to go to university in Winnipeg. Alienated from Manawaka, from Christie and Prin, and even from Jules, she feels she inhabits a different world. This is the beginning of Morag's revolutionary period, which, ironically, leads her into a greater conformity (ultimately, ten lost years she spends married to Brooke). In the end, however, Morag's "revolution" does not work for her.

Notes

Maverick: A dissenter or non-conformist, one who has broken away from the herd. (p. 103)

Browning: Robert Browning (1812-1889) was an English poet renowned for his insight into human mental processes. (p. 121)

pathetic fallacy: Literary term to identify the mistake of attributing human motives and emotions to Nature. (p. 121)

Dieppe: Town in northern France on the English Channel and scene of the controversial Dieppe Raid of August 19, 1942. Of 4,963 Canadian soldiers in the raid, 3,367 were killed or wounded by the Germans. (pp. 143-144)

Bois-Brûlés: French for "Burnt Wood" — the name given to the Métis in the nineteenth century. (p. 145)

The Prophet: Name given to Louis Riel (1844-1885). Riel is one of the great Canadian controversial figures. A madman and fanatic to some, a hero to others, he led the Red River Rebellion of 1869-70 and the North-West Rebellion of 1885. Hanged for treason in 1885, a statue erected on the grounds of the Legislature in Winnipeg now refers to him as the Founder of Manitoba. (pp. 146-147)

Big Bear, Poundmaker: Cree chieftains who fought alongside Riel in the 1885 Rebellion. (p. 148)

Gabriel Dumont: (1838-1906) Riel's chief lieutenant in the North-West Rebellion. After the defeat at Batoche, he escaped to the United States. (p. 148)

Betty Grable: Hollywood star and pin-up queen of World War II. (p. 150)

John Milton: (1608-1674) English poet and statesman, most famous for "On his Blindness" and the epic *Paradise Lost*. (p. 152)

IODE: Imperial Order Daughters of the Empire. Founded in 1900, this English-Canadian patriotic, imperialist and charitable organization is still active. (p. 154)

Rotary Club: A social organization, most of its members are businessmen. (p. 154)

Mea Culpa: Latin for "I am to blame" or "I am guilty." (p. 155)

"This is the Valour of My Ancestors": Motto of the Logan Clan. (p. 162)

"The Ridge of Tears": War cry of the Logan and MacLennan clans. (p. 162)

PART III • CHAPTER 5

Summary

It is morning. Morag, once again caught between the difficulties of getting down to work and her current worries about Pique, looks out over the ruins of the vegetable garden and conjures up her imaginary mentor, the pioneer Catharine Parr Traill. The "discussion" Morag engages in with the invented ghost of Mrs. Traill is interrupted when Royland enters the kitchen. Asked if she is talking to the same lady again, Morag replies that Royland is always catching her at it. But, she insists, it is not because she is alone too much. Surrounded by people, she would still talk to ghosts.

Morag then shows Royland a recent, uninformative post-card from Pique in Vancouver. She reflects that she sometimes understands her daughter, but other times is baffled. Royland tries to reassure Morag. After he leaves, Morag pulls out yesterday's newspaper and rereads an article, looking at the photo accompanying it. Dr. Brooke Skelton has been appointed president of a university. Brooke is still a handsome man.

Memorybank Movie #21 unreels. Morag is leaving Manawaka. Prin seems not to realize what is happening, but tears in her eyes suggest to Morag that maybe she and Christie have never realized how much Prin understands. Morag promises to write, but both she and Christie know she won't.

When the train pulls out of the station, she is exultant. Manawaka is now behind her forever. Suddenly she feels panic. She goes to the washroom to cry, resolute that no one will know what she is feeling inside.

Memorybank Movie #22: Winnipeg. College. The world beyond Manawaka. Morag is a year older than most of the other students, many of whom went to High School together in the city. She feels gawky, insecure, shy and proud at the same time. The concrete sidewalks of the city are alien to her. She is alone, an outsider in a strange land.

She boards with a family in North Winnipeg, far from the downtown university. Her room is like the room she had back in Manawaka — small, cold and barren. Even Morag's meals are similar to those served at Christie and Prin's — plenty of cabbage, wieners and mashed potatoes. It is all like Hill Street, Manawaka, transplanted to the city. Morag feels guilty about wanting to move: Mrs. Crawley has confided in her; the family needs the money.

Winter comes to Winnipeg and Morag catches a cold. Muffled up in bed, studying Milton's *Paradise Lost*, she decides not to return to Manawaka for Christmas. She writes Christie to say she has the flu, wondering all the while if it is merely cowardice on her part. When Christie sends her five dollars, she cries. But she does not relent.

Memorybank Movie #23 introduces Ella Gerson, a Jewish girl in Morag's year who becomes her "friend for life." The two first meet in the office of *Veritas*, the university student paper. Morag has hidden her short story in a book and guesses that Ella, who is holding a copy of Karl Marx's *Das Kapital*, has a submission hidden in *her* book. Morag's guess is right. Ella strikes a dramatic pose and confesses. Neither gets up the nerve to approach one of the office staff regarding their submissions, so they retire to the coffee shop and chat. They agree that a writer has to start somewhere — even if it is a student paper. They show each other some of their work. Ella has written a narrative poem about the Holocaust which is so openly bitter and loving that Morag has difficulty reconciling it with Ella's flippant conversational style. She realizes that Ella, like herself is putting on a mask.

When Morag opens up about her background and the place she now lives in, Ella sympathetically invites her home. First, however, she asks to read Morag's story. Morag is afraid that her work is inferior to Ella's, but Ella's verdict is favourable. Morag feels that Ella will be a life-long friend — someone with whom she can share confidences and talk about herself and her writing.

When she confesses to Ella that she doesn't feel "normal," Ella shrugs it off. "Who wants to be normal?" she asks. Morag passionately admits that she does. She wants to be able to attract men, but can't speak to them as they seem to want to be spoken to. Ella rails against "schmucks" and "phonies" and tells a wry anecdote about meeting a nice boy and then spoiling it by talking about Marx's theory of polarity. Ella sinks into a momentary gloom. She sees no reason why she should pretend to be stupid in order to impress a man. Morag agrees. Nevertheless, she wants to be pretty and glamorous, to get married and have children. *And* she wants to deny all that. "All I want is everything," she concludes.

Morag often goes to the Gerson house now. Mrs. Gerson, who semi-adopts Morag, is the widowed mother of three daughters. The Gerson house radiates a warmth Morag has never known before, which makes her feel like crying. While Ella's sisters, Bernice and Janine, respect Morag's withdrawals to the washroom to cry, Mrs. Gerson marches right in and bluntly tells Morag it is no disgrace to cry. Encouraged by this command, Morag cries. She isn't quite sure why: there are many reasons, all adding up to the fact that she finds life terrifying. Mrs. Gerson, Morag knows, can touch people and hold them, yet still be strong. Morag is strong, but doubts she can reach out to others as the woman who is now holding her can.

Memorybank Movie #24 is called simply, "Brooke."

Morag begins to be asked out by boys she is not really interested in. Generally, when they find out that she lives half-a-mile from the end of the streetcar line, they do not ask her out again.

One evening, Dr. Brooke Skelton greets Morag in the cafeteria and invites her to have coffee with him. He is the awesome professor in her Milton and Seventeenth-Century Poetry courses. Tall and aristocratic, he is regarded by his female students as marvelous. Morag thinks him a prince, but has never dared speak to him outside class. Dr. Skelton says he has just read her story. A copy of *Veritas* is in his hand. Morag grabs the paper from him and sees her name in print — "Fields of Green and Gold" by Morag Gunn. Rapidly and inwardly she criticizes the typographical errors in it, its type, the ending, the story itself. She wonders what her professor thinks of it. Dr. Skelton astounds her by calling it "promising." He says that the ending is sentimental, and Morag quickly agrees. He offers to read and criticize any other fiction she has written.

Morag phones Ella to tell her the news. She then goes up to her room to write a completely unsentimental story, which she realizes is also worthless. She knows that she can't write a story on demand for someone else. She can only write if there is a story that demands telling. This thought humbles her, but she is determined nothing will ever discourage her again.

The next day in class, Dr. Skelton asks Morag to explain an image from a poem by John Donne. She wants to impress him, but when she gets talking, she forgets everything but the image itself.

Later, in Dr. Skelton's office, the professor explains to Morag that he likes her idiomatic expressions. Her directness of speech is refreshing and uncommon in the academic world. When he questions her about her background, Morag is evasive. She is ashamed of her past life and suggests that she doesn't really have one. When he persists in probing her past, she says it is more or less a blank. This comment seems to fascinate her professor, and he offers to drive Morag home.

In the car outside the Crawley's, Brooke Skelton's passionate goodnight kisses make Morag decide that she would do anything for him. He is fourteen years older than she is and insists that she would not be happy with him when she is fifty and he is sixty-four. Morag replies that she is not a child and that she would be happy. Brooke tells her he likes her, despite the fact

46

that she is not beautiful, because of her "mysterious non-existent past." Morag feels as if she is starting life anew. She will conceal everything about herself he might not like.

Morag and Brooke spend more and more time together and are less and less discreet in public. Brooke says he likes her innocence; Morag knows he is mistaken. In his flat, she tries to tell him about herself, but finds she can't. Brooke is quite convinced that Morag is young, innocent and a virgin. When Morag questions how he would feel if she weren't, he says the question does not apply because she is. He makes her promise never to change, to always be happy yet serious. Afterwards, Brooke tells Morag that he has been offered a position at the University of Toronto.

Brooke suggests getting married in the spring and Morag eagerly agrees. But when she brings up the idea of her attending the university, Brooke discourages her, suggesting she might find it awkward when her husband is a professor there. However, if she really wants to, she has a perfect right. She won't need a degree to be a wife. She can sit in on classes or read. After all, getting an education is basically learning and learning how to think. Morag is taken in by all this, and offers no protest. Finally, Brooke suggests she get fitted for a diaphragm because they don't want to have "accidents." Morag knows he means children. She agrees, but adds that she wants his children. Brooke assures her that there'll be lots of time for that — later.

Morag writes to Christie to ask his permission to marry Brooke. She makes various excuses in order not to invite him to the ceremony and concludes by asking after Prin. Christie replies that it is her life and he hopes all goes well. He leaves open the invitation to "Come home when convenient" and adds that Prin is not well.

Memorybank Movie #25 is entitled "Hill Street Revisited." Morag goes back to visit Christie and Prin before she marries and moves to Toronto. It is a depressing visit. The house is the same, only worse. Christie is only fifty-six and looks seventy. Prin is a great hulk in the bed to which she is now confined, her skin the colour of uncooked pastry, her lips puffy, her eyes far away.

When Christie shouts to announce Morag's presence, Prin becomes conscious. Morag asks Christie to leave them alone, and Prin smiles. Morag feels older now. She feels she should stay and look after Prin and Christie, but can't. Morag's announcement of her forthcoming marriage makes Prin giggle.

She sees Morag as eternally young, a little girl.

Morag holds Prin's grotesquely fleshy hand and something strange happens. Prin suddenly reveals that Morag's father did not save Christie's life during World War I. Colin Gunn was just a boy in the war, and, when he would cry, Christie would hold him. Morag considers what Prin has so surprisingly told her. What Christie had told her about her heroic father probably was not the truth. She now believes Prin's story about a boy of eighteen — her father — crying in Christie's arms on the field of battle.

Morag presents Christie with half a bottle of whiskey she has brought him. They drink together silently. When Christie opens his mouth, she fears he will start ranting and raving as in the old days. Instead he merely asks when the wedding will be. She tells him it will be in about two weeks and stumbles over an explanation that no one really will be there. But Christie is not stupid. He reads between the lines and assures her that he would not embarass her by showing up. When Morag tries to deny her meaning, Christie resolutely pours another slug of whiskey and tells her she doesn't need to lie to him.

Morag leaves the next day. When Brooke meets her at the bus depot, she claims that everything was just fine but she missed him and will never leave him again.

Memorybank Movie #26 alludes to Morag's leavetaking from Winnipeg, from university and from Ella. Morag is suddenly frightened as she realizes she will know no one in Toronto except Brooke. She will miss Ella, even though they assure each other that they will write and keep in touch. Morag confesses her nervousness to Ella, who tells her that Brooke is probably nervous too. Morag says he is never nervous, but then wonders. She really doesn't know the man she is going to marry.

Commentary

The theme of faith and works comes through several times in Chapter 5. In the New Testament, the Epistle of James (2:20) says that "faith without works is dead." Morag realizes that writing is hard work and that will power is not enough to get going at it. One must have faith, just as Royland must have faith if he is to divine water. But writing is also work — her work — and a difficult duty.

The theme also emerges in Pique's somewhat cryptic post-card from Vancouver. "This city the end" is an allusion to the Canadian poet Archibald Lampman's nineteenth-century poem, "The City of the End of Things." In this poem, Lampman decries the lifelessness of industrial society in which the works of man are without a soul, without faith. Pique's reference to "Matthew Arnold clash by night right on with this place" alludes to Arnold's nineteenth-century poem "Dover Beach."

In his famous poem, Arnold bemoans the withdrawing of "The Sea of Faith" and appeals to his love for them to "be true to one another" in a world where joy, love and light do not really exist. They exist on "a darkling plain/ Swept with confused alarms of struggle and flight/ Where ignorant armies clash by night."

Pique writes that she and Gord, her present lover, "do not relate so why fight it." She cannot find her place in the sun in Vancouver in a society she finds dark and ignorant, but she has faith in herself. "Am okay, so no dramatics." She will work it out and find who she is and what she must do in life.

As Morag resumes her memorybank movies, we see her leaving Manawaka for Winnipeg. She escapes by train, from which she sees the Nuisance Grounds she feels she is leaving behind forever. But forever is a long time.

Near the end of the chapter, Morag returns to Manawaka to see Christie and Prin before her marriage. Christie advises her not to look back to the dump she has left behind, but says, paradoxically, "It'll all go along with you." Later in her life Morag will write Ella Gerson that "Christie knew things about inner truths that I am only beginning to understand."

Ella, whom she meets at university in Winnipeg, is a kindred spirit. She is the first friend of Morag's who is also a writer and the first friend who becomes a sister. Ella's mother makes Morag feel at home for the first time. Warmth and intelligence, strength and vulnerability are combined in this woman. She and Ella become role models for Morag and increase her sense of social awareness.

The play *Hamlet* contains the famous lines, spoken by Polonius to his son Laertes: "This above all: to thine own self be true,/ And it must follow as the night the day,/ Thou cans't not then be false to any man." As has been noted, the war-cry Morag will adopt in middle age is "Gainsay who Dare."

Yet, in this chapter, while *trying* to become more herself,

Morag denies herself. She does not want to downgrade herself for any man, yet she does for Dr. Brooke Skelton, the English professor she is prepared to marry by the end of the chapter. She denies university, her past, her sexual experience, her own physical appearance, her adopted parents, and ultimately she denies herself. She is not exactly being true to herself. How then can she be true to any man?

Brooke sweeps her off her feet. He is a prince to her. She will be brand new for him, because that is what he wants. It is well to consider the Pygmalion theme from ancient Greek myth here. In the myth, Pygmalion creates a beautiful marble statue with which he falls in love. He prays to Aphrodite, the goddess of love, to turn her into a woman, Galatea. He is in love with his own creation. So it is with Brooke, who basically denies that Morag is a real woman and a real person.

Morag's marriage is a mistake she will later regret. Brooke cannot give of himself. When she forgoes her university education to move to Toronto with him, he says that really education is learning how to think. This may well be true, but he is determined to be her *sole* teacher. Morag falls under his spell. Brooke wants to assert his power over her, and for his sake she largely denies her own power. What she earlier told Ella, "All I want is everything," is denied, or at least suppressed, in her ten years with Dr. Skelton.

The chapter ends, as do so many chapters in the book, with a leave-taking. Morag goes to Toronto — a city she comes to fear and hate. But she will survive.

Notes

Jerusalem: Ancient capital and holy city of Israel. Sion (Zion) is the hill in Jerusalem where King Solomon's temple was built. (p. 169)

The Book of Job: In the Old Testament, this book deals with the unmerited sufferings of Job, who takes God to task and demands to know *why*. (p. 170)

Gerard Manley Hopkins: English priest and innovative poet (1844-1889) of the late Victorian period, who was not published until the twentieth century. (p. 171)

Matthew Arnold: English poet and critic (1822-1888). (p. 171)

Garden: In the Book of Genesis, the Garden of Eden is the original home of Adam and Eve before they sinned and were cast out into the world by God. The Garden is thus a symbol for our Paradise Lost. John Milton's seventeenth century epic poem *Paradise Lost* seeks to justify God's ways to man, to explain man's fall from innocence and his loss of Eden. (p. 178)

Das Kapital: (*Capital*) Book by Karl Marx (1818-1883) which criticizes the capitalist system. (p. 178)

Sarah Bernhardt: French actress (1844-1923) known for her exaggerated dramatic gestures. (p. 178)

Veritas: Latin word for "truth". (p. 178)

Auschwitz, Buchenwald: German concentration camps run by the Nazis during World War II where millions of Jews were murdered in what has come to be known as the Holocaust. (p. 179)

Lumpen proletariat: Anti-social urban poor from whom no class solidarity can be expected in the battle against capitalism. The term was coined by Karl Marx. (p. 180)

schmuck: Yiddish (i.e. German-Jewish) word for a jerk. (p. 181)

schlemiel: Yiddish word for a bumbling fool or a gullible person. (p. 181)

metaphysical image: A subtle and complex figure of speech which startles by its comparison of two seemingly unlike things. It was common in the so-called metaphysical poetry of John Donne and his contemporaries. (p. 190)

jezebel: A wicked, scheming, loose woman, named after the wife of King Ahab of Israel in the Old Testament. A faithless hussy. (p. 201).

"The voice of the turtle is heard in the land": Famous quotation from the Old Testament (Song of Solomon 2:12). In ancient Israel, the appearance of the turtle dove was a herald of spring. (p. 209)

CHAPTER 6

Summary
Morag sits in her big, comfy armchair by the kitchen window with a glass of scotch. She is celebrating the receipt of a royalty cheque the day before. "Stand fast" — the motto inscribed on the label of the scotch bottle — makes her wonder why all the Scottish mottoes are so grim and resolute. Thinking

of the Logan crest with the pierced heart makes her realize that she misses Christie, who has now been dead for seven years.

Needing to talk, Morag phones Ella in Toronto. Ella, now married for the second time, is the mother of five-year-old twins. She has had four books of poetry published and is working on a fifth book. She tells Morag she is fine but has the feeling of living "too many lives simultaneously." This is a feeling Morag can share.

Morag announces that Pique is coming home, but has split up with Gord. She wonders if her daughter will have the same pattern of unstable relationships as her mother. Ella assures Morag that an inability to form lasting relationships is not passed on with the genes and invites her friend to visit Toronto. But Morag says she is trying to write: "I always thought it would get easier, but it doesn't," she says. Ella agrees.

Morag feels cheered up. She thanks Ella, says goodbye, pours another scotch, and sits looking out over the river, wondering how Brooke would remember their years together. His memories would be different from hers, she concludes.

Memorybank Movie #27 takes her back to Toronto. She is afraid of the noise, the cars and the unfamiliarity of the city. Brooke laughs at her when she clutches his arm in the street, but he is pleased. When they sit in their livingroom, she reads quietly so as not to disturb him while he is marking papers. She spends most of her time reading or listening.

One evening, Morag decides she wants to know more about Brooke's past. He has not been back to India since he was sixteen, and, when he does talk about it, there seems to be a note of homesickness in his voice. She wants to know everything about him and tries to imagine the house he lived in.

Brooke remembers the poverty of India. He believes that the passing of the British Raj — British sovereignty — was not a good thing for India. This opinion apalls Morag, who dislikes imperialism and the wide discrepancy between rich and poor, the colonials and the colonized. When Brooke suggests that his "little one" doesn't know what it was like — doesn't understand that there is no real justice in the world — his patronizing tones make her change the subject.

What were his parents like? His mother is a shadow in Brooke's mind, always restrained and quiet. His father was "difficult" recalls Brooke, who tells how, as a child, he once had to sit on a trunk outside the gates of the family home, wearing a sign that read "I Am Bad." Brooke does not remember why his father punished him so humiliatingly, but his father finally had to relent, for young Brooke did not apologize nor did he cry. The experience taught Brooke to stand up for himself, a quality which served him well when he was later sent to a military boarding school in England. Determined not to be pushed around, Brooke worked his way up to "Sergeant" at the age of eight. Brooke forces a grin in recalling his past, but says he was determined never to become like his father. Morag denies that Brooke could ever be harsh. His students adore him, and so does she.

When they make love, Morag feels they are truly together. The possibility of their having a child, however, is a subject Brooke does not want to discuss. One night she wakens him from a nightmare in which he kept repeating the word "Minoo." When she presses him to know who "Minoo" refers to, Brooke claims not to know, and impatiently demands that she let him sleep. Morag is left awake, thinking about Brooke and his inability to communicate with her.

Memorybank Movie #28 features Morag at twenty-four. After four years in Toronto, she is still intimidated by the city, although she will not admit it. She knows her way around the bookstores and the university. She knows how to pick out clothes that will please Brooke, she watches her figure carefully, and she has her hair fashionably short and permed — as Brooke likes it. She is the model housewife. But beneath it all, Morag is frustrated. She tries to write short stories, but tears them up. One day she hurls an Indian ashtray through the window. She arranges for the window to be replaced, pays the repairman and shreds the bill down the toilet — without telling Brooke.

Brooke's obvious determination not to have a child prompts Morag to confront him petulantly. The discussion ends with her apologizing. She begs him never to leave her. Brooke's promise to be with her and to protect her always makes Morag feel uneasy.

When Morag suggests that she find a job, Brooke encourages her to work at writing. Morag admits that she has not given it up, but that everything turns out badly. Brooke asks that *he* be the judge of that. At his request, Morag shows him some stories. Brooke commends them. He suggests that they need polishing but are definitely worth working on. Although eager for approval, Morag disagrees. He is suprised by her appraisal of them as "trivial and superficial."

Some of Brooke's Third Year students come over in the evening. Morag observes Brooke being supportive and friendly, but never trying to be one of them. His criticisms are gentle. When one student suggests that some of the poetry of Gerard Manley Hopkins is intentionally obscure, Morag jumps heatedly into the discussion. But then she stops, realizing that she has said too much, that she has slipped out of her role as dutiful wife and silent partner.

Later she apologizes to Brooke, who reassures his "child" that everyone makes overstatements from time to time. The word "child" makes Morag draw away in protest. However, Brooke's comments on her touchiness find her, once again, apologizing to him.

Memorybank Movie #29 is titled "Spear of Innocence." That is also the title of Morag's first novel, which she writes during this "movie." The novel takes Morag by surprise as it comes to life on paper. She wrestles with her characterization of the novel's heroine, Lilac Stonehouse, a small-town girl who goes to the big city. Morag is writing the novel in the third person — but from Lilac's viewpoint. This presents difficulties to Morag, for Lilac's character must be presented through her words and actions, and Lilac frequently does not understand herself. How to get this across to the reader? Morag feels she *is* getting it across — but only while she is writing. When she stops, she has doubts.

Brooke suggests that they go out to a movie. Morag consents, even though she would actually rather stay home and work on her novel. She realizes she is lying to Brooke (when she says she'd love to see a movie) and that she has done it before.

That evening, Brooke is depressed — he wonders aloud to Morag whether teaching makes any difference and whether he ever makes contact with any of his students. As she offers assurances, Morag is struck by how she once thought Brooke completely confident. Brooke reveals that his dream would be to run a tea plantation in India. However, he would not go there again, he says, because he would not feel at home anymore. Morag sees her husband as trapped in an imaginative garden which has no external counterpart. For her it is different. She would never return to Manawaka, yet Manawaka is in her mind. Morag wishes she could do something to help Brooke.

That night, Brooke is again droning "Minoo" in his sleep. Morag wakes him and asks him to tell her about his dream. Brooke reveals that Minoo was his *ayah* or nursemaid in India. His own mother was distant and unaffectionate; Minoo used to play with him — and sometimes comforted him at night, when he couldn't sleep. One night, Brooke's father came into the bedroom. That was why he beat Brooke and put him on the trunk outside, wearing the "I Am Bad" sign.

Brooke claims that it is a "nuisance" that this incident from his childhood keeps coming back to him. Although he always hated his father, he did learn to be tough, to run his life his own way, and to keep a firm control over things.

After this revelation, Morag ventures to say that in spite of having been married for 5 years, they still barely know each other. It's time they started talking to each other, and sharing their past. She suggests: "I'm not the way you think I am. And you're not the way I thought you were, either." But Brooke dismisses her appeal, reminding her that he has an early morning class and must get some sleep.

Morag usually stops writing at four o'clock so that she can prepare dinner for Brooke. One day, however, she is so absorbed with a problem involving Lilac that Brooke arrives before she is ready. Morag is chain-smoking and trembling, and Brooke wonders what is wrong. When she says that *she* is all right, but that her novel's character has run into a problem, he laughs, relieved: "I thought you'd been suddenly stricken with something serious." Morag wants to say that the problem *is* serious. (It involves Lilac having a self-induced abortion.) But the problem is in her imaginative world, not in the so-called "real" world, and she cannot talk about it. It is real to her. Brooke would not understand. He tells her to get dressed so they can go out for dinner.

Commentary

The Diviners is a carefully-structured novel. The end of one chapter usually connects with the beginning of the next, even though chapters end in the fade-out of a memorybank movie and begin in the continuing present. Chapter 5 ends with Morag leaving university, Winnipeg, and Ella. On the second page of

Chapter 6, Morag is a successful writer in her home on the river who feels lonely for Christie — now dead — and for Ella — a succesful writer in Toronto. So she phones Ella. Morag's past and present are thus linked together, both in memory and in everyday practical reality.

In her writing, Laurence paints a big canvas, but she also commands the precise and telling details. They are interesting and pointed enough in themselves, but they also link up with other details elsewhere and have the kind of significance which repays the reader on each re-reading of the novel. For example, as the chapter opens, Morag is drinking Glenfiddich Scotch, a pure malt whiskey which is very expensive. She has received a royalty cheque the day before and is celebrating. Morag considers it might be a "Thanksgiving celebration, as the case might be. The case," she muses. "Did anybody actually buy scotch by the case?" By this means we are shown the way Morag's mind habitually works — by association. We have the feeling of actually being inside her head, following along the labyrinthine and often amusing paths her mind takes in its daily operations.

When she resumes her memorybank movies, we are in Toronto with her and her new husband. Morag's life is quiet and largely subordinated to his, but she is learning and observing, absorbing, digesting and assimilating material. All this will become the stuff of the novels she has yet to begin to write.

She still pretends she has no past and yet is eager to know more about Brooke's life. He grew up in India, he is English and he is educated. So his life seems more exotic, more interesting and more important than her own. It is not merely coincidental that the first memorybank movie in this chapter is called "Raj Mataj." The title suggests "razzmatazz" — a lot of showily impressive stuff; "Raj" is the Hindi word for "ruler" and suggests the days of British colonialism in India. Of course, Brooke is Morag's prince and ruler. She is like a colony to him, subordinate and underdeveloped — an unknown country.

Laurence has commented on many occasions that she perceives a relationship between the status of women and colonial countries. (Canada should identify more with the countries of the Third World, she believes, instead of comparing itself to the United States, France and Britain. And women should stop comparing themselves unfavourably to men.) Christie warned Morag that if she allowed herself to be a doormat, everyone

56

would step on her. Individuals, peoples, countries who deny themselves will be exploited. Such relationships are not good ones, for they do not admit of the integrity, equality and freedom necessary for healthy relationships which can evolve and grow.

Brooke wants to be the judge of Morag's writing and does not trust her to judge herself. He does not want a child, although Morag desparately wants one by him. To him, she is his "little one" — a term of endearment he insists. But it is fairly clear that he sees her as a child, his child, and not as an adult and an equal.

Morag believes he loves her and she him. But since neither really knows the other, her judgement must be questioned. Who is it he loves? Who is it she loves? Trust and respect seem to be lacking in their marriage.

When Morag begins writing her first novel, Brooke cautions her that she is setting her sights high, for the novel is a complex structure. This is not exactly encouragement. Then Brooke suggests they go out to a movie. Morag would rather stay home and write, but dutifully goes with Brooke because that is what is expected of her. Again, she is denying herself. But now, at least, she realizes that she is lying to Brooke when she says she'd "love" to go. She is surprised to suddenly realize that she has been lying to him for a long time. Also, her "will" to always be happy and cheerful for Brooke makes her wonder, for the first time — "if this act of willing, however willingly undertaken, is false to her, can it be true to Brooke?"

Later that night, when Morag thinks she would never go back to Manawaka, she realizes for the first time that the town nonetheless "inhabits her, as once she inhabited it." Even though she has not yet come to terms with it, her past, which she sought so long to deny, lives on inside her.

Notes

Raj: Hindi word for rule, sovereignty. (p. 217)

Assam: State in north-eastern India, renowned for its tea. (p. 227)

Black Celt: The Celts were the ancient Britons and Gauls from whom, in part, Morag is descended. Black suggests the gloom and dark moodiness of the people. (p. 227)

CHAPTER 7

Summary

After spending the day working on her novel, Morag takes a walk along the rutted country road near her house. When she returns, she is relieved to discover that Pique is back, hungry and looking much the same, wearing a belt with an old brass buckle that seems oddly familiar to Morag. The belt and buckle are, in fact, from Jules.

Pique had a good trip. She was scared, however, by the hostility shown by some people on the road who, she sensed, feared her for being different and rejecting the middle-class way of life. She is not quite ready to talk about her visit to Manawaka. The town has changed, she thinks, although perhaps it is the same underneath. She remarks that tacky little houses now litter Hill Street and Christie's house seems no longer to be there. When Morag asks if Pique went down to the valley, she resists answering and instead resumes eating. The best thing about the trip was that Jules had given Pique some of his songs. This means a lot to Pique, who needs to know if her mother *loved* her father and why, after all, she was born.

Morag finds it impossible to convey in one phrase the complexity of her feelings for Jules. Pique is close to tears when she says that her father is losing his voice and finding it harder to get jobs singing. He has only one thing to exploit, and that remains unspoken. Morag knows it is his being half-Indian. She confesses that sometimes she would like to see Jules, but wonders if he would feel the same. Pique explodes: "You're so goddamn proud and so scared of being rejected."

Just as they are about to prepare dinner, Gord comes in — at which point Pique leaves to avoid any confrontation. He is confused and tries to persuade Morag to tell him what Pique wants. Morag can only suggest that she must be left alone for awhile. Pique herself is unsure of what she wants her life to be. It is a journey which is as yet incomplete.

The next morning Royland brings a fish for Pique's breakfast and wonders if Pique would like to go divining that afternoon. While waiting for Pique to wake up, the old man tells Morag a little about his past life — of how he had been a preacher, and had driven his wife to suicide with his fanaticism.

Later on, the Smiths come by to introduce their visitor,

Dan Scranton. He and Pique seem to establish an instant rapport. He plays the guitar and sings songs about his native Alberta; Pique brings out her guitar and sings a song written by Louis Riel. When Morag asks where she learned it, Pique replies brusquely that she got if from a book. Someone had to teach her the sounds of the French words. She resents not knowing what they mean. Morag, that night, softly plays an old record called "Morag of Dunvegin." The words are in Gaelic, which she does not understand, but she listens as if listening would in itself make them comprehensible. She thinks of all the people she has known who have lost the language of their ancestors: of old fishermen in Crombruach, Scotland, who spoke a lovely English as if they were translating their thoughts from the Gaelic; of Christie telling his tales in English with just a vague echo of Scots in his voice. She thinks of Jules who has lost two languages — French and Cree — and who had only English as a foreign language. She remembers that Brooke had spoken Hindi as a child, but forgot most of it later. It is sad to lose a language, she thinks. Musing on Brooke's loss of a language not his own, Morag starts up Memorybank Movie #30, "Frictions."

It begins with what has become Brooke's standard phrase before he has sex with Morag: "Have you been a good girl, love?" If she does not play along with it, he angrily refuses any involvement with her.

Brooke is now head of the English Department. In keeping with his new status, the Skelton apartment is stylish, furnished in Danish Modern. Morag writes during the day while Brooke is out. She finally finishes her first novel. It has taken three years and she feels empty. When Brooke learns she is finished, he offers to read it so he can make useful suggestions. Morag agrees but first wants to discuss the matter of having a child. Brooke always seeks to avoid the subject. He suggests it is not a world one would want to bring children into. Morag drops the subject.

Reluctantly she shows *Spear of Innocence* to her husband. When he offers his critical suggestions, she says she'll think about them. Instead, she sends off the manuscript to a publisher the next day without telling Brooke.

Memorybank Movie #31 takes Morag back to Manawaka to see the dying Prin. Christie meets Morag at the station. He tells her that Prin is not long for this world — a phrase that strikes Morag as uncharacteristic. Morag feels guilty for having deserted the Logans and leaving Christie to look after Prin alone. Christie looks terrible. At sixty-four he is as ancient as a fossil.

That night, in her old room, Morag feels haunted by ghosts from her real and imagined past. Young Morag, Piper Gunn, Rider Tonnerre — all seem a blend of the real and imaginary.

Prin is in the hospital. She would rather die at home; but there, Christie cannot possibly care for her needs. Morag guiltily offers to look after Prin, but the doctor will not release her and Christie will not fight to grant Prin's wish. Those days are past. Prin lies huge and quiet, shrouded by her bedsheets. Her face is blank, her eyes are open but unseeing. She is unaware of Morag's presence. Two days later, she dies.

Christie and Morag hold a wake together over a bottle of Scotch. Christie ponders the paradox that Prin always seemed simultaneously old and young to him. He says that he believed always that she was "kind of simple in the head." Morag implies that perhaps she was not retarded, but simple like a child. Christie does not grasp the distinction. He sits shrunken and diminished by the death of his wife. He feels that he had been a hard man to live with. There was in him that element of the Celtic gloom which Prin could not understand. Morag tells him that Prin's life would have been much worse without Christie, but Christie is not sure.

Eleven people attend Prin's funeral. Eva Winkler is there. She chats briefly with Morag, telling her that the little brother, Vern, is now grown up. He has moved to Vancouver and adopted the name Thor Thorlakson. Morag thanks Eva for all she did for Prin and feels guilty when Eva insists it was nothing compared with the goodness Prin showed her and Vern. The simple Service for the Burial of the Dead concludes with Prin's favourite hymn, which Morag had requested. "Jerusalem the Golden" contains the lines from which the title of Part Three is taken: "those halls of Sion." As Morag takes Christie's arm to go to the graveyard, Christie mumbles that he would have buried Prin in the Nuisance Grounds.

Memorybank Movie #32: "The Tower." Morag is back in Toronto. Her apartment high above the city seems a desert island, a cave, a tower. Increasingly, she feels isolated and cut off from life. The city is boring. Her only contact with the outside world is through letters from Ella in Halifax. Ella counsels patience, reassures her and curses the publishers for not responding to Morag's manuscript.

Brooke's worshipful English seminar students seem bland to Morag. Thinking of Rapunzel in the fairytale tower who let down her hair to let the prince climb up, Morag decides literally to let down her hair. When she stops going to the hairdresser, Brooke does not approve. He tells her that her hair is a mess. Morag is adamant. She can no longer tolerate people making her into something she is not — not even for Brooke.

Brooke is disturbed by Morag's rebellion. He suggests that his "little one" is getting worked up over nothing. When Morag rejects his affections, he demands to know what is wrong. As she pleads with him not to call her "little one," Morag's suppressed anger is released in a flood of words which are in Christie's language and not her own. Brooke attributes the abnormal outburst to hysteria, and asks Morag if she is due to menstruate. Brooke thinks that Morag is rejecting his affection. "Little one" expresses caring; it is not a put-down, he avers. Morag cannot argue. She tries to explain that she never really was treated as a kid when she was young. She doesn't know how to deal with his phrase and all it implies.

Brooke now blames the whole outburst on her return to Manawaka rousing bad memories she had forgotten. When he asks her to simply dismiss it from her mind, Morag boldly asserts that she had never forgotten any of her past. "It was always there," she states. Brooke is disillusioned. He liked the idea that Morag had no past, that she was starting life brand-new with him.

Morag apologizes for unintentionally deceiving Brooke. She is not the person he thinks she is. But Brooke cannot part with his image of Morag and is convinced that if Morag will just get her hair fixed and not think about her past in Manawaka, everything will be fine.

After the first publisher rejects Morag's novel, she sends it to another. The second publisher is interested, but wants revisions. Morag looks at the manuscript for the first time in almost a year. She finds some of the editorial comments relevant, and begins rewriting parts of the novel. To her surprise, Morag finds she can defend it. She is no longer personally involved with it. She makes the necessary changes and then tells Brooke.

He greets her news that the novel has been accepted with surprise and pleasure, then asks if they want any changes made. Morag's rejection of his offer to take a look at her manuscript results in a rather sarcastic attack. He curtly suggests that she might like to take over his Fourth-Year Contemporary Novel course.

Morag is more furious than she has been in years. Without thinking, she picks up a glass bowl and heaves it at the fireplace. Brooke is icily controlled. In a superior tone, he advises her to clear up the pieces and not to do it again. Since she objects to being treated as a child, he suggests she should stop acting like one. Morag agrees. She is stunned by what she has done and apologizes. This time Brooke simply announces wearily that he won't want dinner and is going into his study to mark papers.

When the reviews for *Spear of Innocence* arrive they are mixed. Even the good ones often seem to be dealing with a novel other than the one Morag wrote. Brooke is not pleased that she has chosen to use her own name — Morag Gunn — on the cover. He wonders aloud if she didn't think it worth taking the chance to put her married name on it.

Morag wants to leave Brooke but does not see how she can. She can't even tell Ella. She walks blankly through the streets of the city, distant and despairing. One day, thus preoccupied, she sees Jules Tonnerre coming out of a rooming house. She runs up to him and hugs him. It is almost ten years since they last saw each other. They chat and go for coffee. Jules is now a country and western singer in bars around Ontario and Quebec. He sings some of his own songs too: "Maybe they're crap as well, but at least it's my own crap," he says. He does not make much money, but thinks it is better than working in a factory.

Morag invites Jules for dinner. While she is preparing the meal, they drink scotch, and Jules tells Morag about Billy Joe, his partner, who plays guitar along with him. He laughs that he has to dress up in phoney satin shirts with lots of beadwork when he plays the bars. That's what the audience wants from an Indian.

When Brooke arrives home, he does not shake hands with Jules, but goes into the bathroom. He calls Morag in and accuses Jules of freeloading, and Morag of having her past catch up with her. He reminds her that two of his friends are coming for dinner and that Jules can't stay. He adds that it is illegal to give liquor to Indians.

Jules, who has overheard, grins and leaves. Morag grabs her bag and coat, and follows him. In Jules' dismal room, Morag unwinds. She blames no one. She and Brooke were playing a game — and some of it was good — but she can't play it anymore because she is different now. Morag announces that she intends to leave Brooke. She spends the night with Jules.

In the morning, Morag realizes, despite Jules' advice, that she will have to go back to the apartment and tell Brooke she is leaving. She feels she can't go back to Manawaka and decides to head out to the coast. Jules offers to let her stay with him until she gets things straightened out. She accepts his offer and lets him know she won't stay for long.

When she arrives at her old apartment door, she is shaking with fright. Brooke, who has been crying, is sitting in his study. Morag apologizes. She can't explain why she stayed with Jules; she will take from their bank account the money she earned from her novel and leave for Vancouver. She tells him she'll do anything necessary for a divorce. After a few more words, neither she nor Brooke have anything to say. He goes back to marking essays. Morag packs a suitcase and leaves.

When Morag returns to Jules, she asks if he would mind if she didn't use birth control. Jules laughs and calls her a crazy woman, but says he doesn't need to give her permission. He reiterates that she can stay with him until she is ready to move to Vancouver. Morag stays for just over three weeks.

She leaves with a one-way ticket to Vancouver and five hundred dollars. On the train she vomits. Tidying up after herself, it suddenly strikes her that she might be pregnant. Briefly she panics and wonders where Brooke is. She thinks about the distances between them as the train moves across the prairies, westward bound.

Commentary

The descriptive passages in *The Diviners* warrant careful consideration; for what may often appear at first reading to be merely incidental turns out to be revealing in any number of ways.

The description of the swallows is a case in point. The fledglings are ready to fly, and Morag assures the parents that she is "no threat to your young." Then she enters her house to discover that Pique is back. Her "fledgling" who left the nest to find her wings, has returned. Pique tells her mother about her adventures, but holds back on some of the details. They chat while Pique eats, then argue, and Pique cries out against her mother's quibbling over words. Then there is silence, which is broken by the sound of the young sparrows still in their nest outside, "wanting to fly." The relationship between the young sparrows and Pique, the nest and the house, leaving and returning — all these relationships of parent and young, freedom and maturity are implicit in this passage for the reader to discover.

Pique is wearing her father's belt and buckle and has learnt some of his songs. She is an inheritor, glad to have a connection, through her father, with her Métis past, but not yet conscious of *why* these things have value for her. Pique doesn't read books, so Morag wonders what she can give her daughter as her heritage. This sense of essential continuity and tradition was first set off in the novel by the epigraph from Al Purdy: "but they had their being once/ and left a place to stand on" and follows through to the concluding pages.

When Pique starts singing, in French, the song Louis Riel wrote in jail before he was hanged, she does not understand the meaning of the words. She does not speak the language of that side of her family. We are reminded of how often in the novel Morag bemoans the loss of a language. Jules has lost most of his Cree and French, Christie has lost the Gaelic of his ancestors and Brooke has forgotten Hindi. Morag, always entranced by the powerful music of words, longs to know her ancestral Gaelic, but it remains a mystery to her. Knowing and understanding a common language that one's forefathers spoke is an essential link with one's past. A language is a prime means of being a people, of an individual's being part of a larger community.

Morag feels the same sense of regret when she returns to Manawaka for Prin's funeral and finds that the aging Christie remembers telling the younger Morag the stories that so charged her, but can no longer remember what they were about or what they meant to them both. Then, after returning to Toronto and fighting with Brooke, Morag explodes in Christie's language. It is at this point that she tells her shocked husband she has *not* forgotten her past: "It was always there."

This recognition on the part of Morag is in fact a reassertion of herself. It is a bold, if unconsciously provoked, declaration of her freedom and foreshadows her break from the artificial present in which she has been living with Brooke.

Brooke, on the contrary, believes naively that if you ignore problems, they will go away. This is not true: his disturbed past emerges in his dreams of Minoo and his father. He is a haunted man who can recognize neither the past nor the present. His difficulties with Morag will not go away simply because he refuses to realize them. His romantic vision of a brave new world is not based on a sense of the past or an intimation of the future. Rather, he chooses to shut out his father and he chooses not to have a child. He will not grow up, but Morag will.

Having her name, Morag Gunn, printed on the cover of her first novel is a further assertion of Morag's individuality and freedom. Why did she choose that name? "It goes a long way back," she tells her disappointed husband. The cover design of *Spear of Innocence* goes back a long way, too. The spear piercing a valentine heart is a vulgarized version of Christie's family crest: A passion nail piercing a human heart, proper.

The publication of this first novel — without any assistance from Brooke — does not help the marriage. If Morag can make it on her own, then what is Brooke's value? To a man who sees the world largely in terms of possession, power and control, Morag's independent success is a threat to his dominance.

Morag's chance reunion with Jules on the street leads to the final break with Brooke. She brings Jules back to the apartment for a drink. When Brooke insults Jules (who is used to it), he also insults Morag. She leaves with Jules and stays overnight. When she returns to the apartment in the morning to pick up her things, she sees Brooke a broken man, She knows she will never live under his domination again.

For three weeks Morag lives with Jules. Jules accuses her of using him as a "shaman" to break Brooke's spell. The word is appropriate: it is used only in connection with one other character in the novel — Royland. He divines for hidden sources of water with his divining rod; Jules finds hidden sources in Morag with his lovemaking; Morag divines hidden truths with her pen. All three are diviners, or magicians of sorts. The act of sex with Jules releases Morag from her bondage to Brooke.

Morag, with Jules' consent, chooses to have a child by him. And so Pique is conceived, a blending of three of Canada's solitudes — Scots, French, Indian. But there will be no marriage.

Pique's earlier outburst at her mother in Chapter 7 is, in part, justified. "Why did you have me?" she screamed, accusing Morag of conceiving her for Morag's own reasons and without consideration for Jules or for her. Morag could not know the difficulties that Pique's mixed heritage would bring her.

This chapter, and Part Three, ends with Morag again leaving on a train. This time she is heading out west, passing Manawaka on the way to Canada's Pacific Coast, where she will try to make a new life. And she is bringing a new life with her within her womb.

Notes
anthropomorphically: (adverb) In the form of a human. (p. 242)

Crombruach: Village in Ross-shire in the northern Scottish Highlands where the McRaiths live. (p. 244)

Cree: Amerindian tribe and a dialect of the Algonkian language group. The Crees are indigenous to Northern Ontario and central Saskatchewan and Manitoba. Galloping Mountain would be in Cree territory. (p. 244)

Rapunzel: Heroine of one of Grimm's Fairy Tales. Imprisoned in a tower, she lets down her long golden hair to permit a prince to climb up to her. (p. 255)

protean: Variable, capable of taking on many different forms. Proteus was a character in Greek mythology who could readily transform himself. (p. 255)

Beulah Land: Israel; a land of perpetual peace. (p. 256)

Mazeltov: Hebrew for congratulations. (p. 261)

shaman: A wise old man of the tribe who has special contact with the divine; a magician of sorts. (p. 273; p. 451)

The Coast: The West Coast; British Columbia (p. 276)

Lear: King Lear in Shakespeare's tragedy of the same name. Lear felt himself "more sinned against than sinning." (pp. 277-278)

PART IV • CHAPTER 8

Summary

It is August, and Pique and Dan are living together with Morag. They stay up all night and sleep during the day, reversing what Morag perceives as the natural order of life. She had agreed to their living with her, but she is resentful. The young lovers worked for a while and are living off their earnings, so they do not impose themselves on Morag financially. In addition, they do more than their share of the housework. Nevertheless, Morag goes around each morning slamming doors, stomping about the kitchen and creating noise. It is something other than their hours that disturbs her.

When Royland drops by, she reveals her guilt over her attitude toward Pique and Dan. Royland understands the real reason for Morag's moodiness, and she admits it: she is 47, alone — and likely to be alone for the rest of her life. Despite the fact that, for the most part, this is the way she wants it, she is jealous of the happiness of the young couple. Royland helps her to realize that if she explains her feelings to Pique and Dan, she might feel better.

When Morag tells the two exactly how she feels, Dan and Pique respond that they had thought it was something like that, and they understand. Dan says that they have decided to live with the Smiths across the river. They'll visit often. Morag will not be deserted.

Later, Morag writes a letter to her friend Dan McRaith, in Scotland. "Dear McRaith —" she begins, and explains that she cannot call him "Dan" anymore because of Pique's Dan. She would like to call the latter by some other name, but that would necessitate awkward explanations. Morag's letter leads into Memorybank Movie #33: "Bleak House."

Morag is pregnant and alone, living in a boarding house in the Kitsilano area of Vancouver. People who cannot afford to live elsewhere live here in Kitsilano, she thinks. One morning Mrs. Maggie Tefler, Morag's landlady, hears Morag vomiting in the sink. She brusquely guesses that Morag is pregnant and suggests that she go back to her husband.

When Morag refuses to confirm that the child is not her husband's, Mrs. Tefler proposes that Morag take a room in the attic in exchange for doing the housework. Morag, who has little choice, accepts with thanks. Despite the low rafters, Morag likes her room. At least it is her own. She buys odds and ends to fix it up comfortably. She recalls the famous dictum of Virginia Woolf that a woman, if she is to write, must have "a room of one's own." And that is what she has . . . even if she writes little because the pregnancy wears her out.

Memorybank Movie #34: "Portrait of the Artist as a

Pregnant Skivvy.'' Morag is four months pregnant now when Mrs. Tefler brings her a long-expected letter addressed to Mrs. Brooke T. Skelton. Morag has written Brooke to tell him she is using her own name now, but she has not told him of her pregnancy.

Needless to say, the letter is patronizing. Morag has proved her point and he will try to forget her silly action if she wants to come home and act sensibly. He will send the train fare. Morag is torn: he has come as close as he can to admitting his need for her; she needs him too. But there is no going back. She wonders if she got pregnant to ensure that she could not return to Brooke. Did she choose Jules as a father so that no one could think the child was Brooke's? Has she betrayed the unborn child along with everyone else?

Morag writes to Brooke. In reply, she gets a letter from his lawyer, seeking a doctor's confirmation of her pregnancy, a legal document stating that Brooke is not the father, and the name of the father along with the dates of the adulteries. Morag complies with the first two demands, but refuses to implicate Jules.

One evening Morag is visited by Hank Masterson, the local representative of her publishers, Walton and Pierce. He brings the news that *Spear of Innocence* has been accepted by publishers in the United States and England. That will mean more money for Morag, who is almost broke. Masterson encourages her to write and suggests she do some articles for the local paper. He will get her a literary agent.

The new agent, Milward Crispin, succeeds in selling one of Morag's stories. The money from this and from her English and American royalties enables Morag to give up the housework and simply rent the room. Mrs. Tefler thinks ''it must be nice to be able to earn a living just sitting there.'' Morag does not argue.

Memorybank Movie #35: ''Voices from Past Places'' introduces someone from Morag's Manawaka past. Julie Kazlik, whom Morag has not seen for ten years, has read Morag's articles in the paper and discovered her address.

Exchanging news, Morag reveals she has left her husband. Julie retorts that she is leaving *her* husband too, because he is ''loco.'' She'll leave him and take her two-year-old son to Montreal where she intends to marry Dennis, a nice guy in insurance.

Julie suggests that since she is moving to Montreal, Morag move into her old apartment — she has the top floor of a friend's house in North Vancouver.

Memorybank Movie #36 features the birth of Pique. Morag has never been in the antiseptic world of a hospital before. The cold voice of the nurse who advises her not to advertise her unmarried state does not make Morag feel more comfortable. The labour pains continue until the baby is born. Morag demands to hold her child: Piquette Tonnerre Gunn.

Morag finds, however, that she cannot call her child Piquette, so she shortens it to Pique. When the baby is two months old, Morag gets Julie to take a roll of colour film. She sends one picture of the baby, with a note, to Jules, who replies that he is pleased with Morag's choice of name for her. He is still moving about, singing, but hopes to see his daughter some day.

Morag finds she can no longer type much now that she has a baby. She starts writing in longhand. Two of her stories have been sold, but the editors have shown no interest in her Piper Gunn tales. She longs for more money.

Mrs. Tefler makes unflattering remarks about Pique's looks and ancestry. Christie writes that he would like to see the baby and hopes it looks like Morag. The lawyers let her know that she is no longer Mrs. Brooke Skelton. Then Julie phones to say her divorce has come through and she is moving to Montreal.

Memorybank Movie #37 refers to Morag's new address in North Vancouver: Begonia Road. Mrs. Tefler does not respond kindly to Morag's sudden move and ends up calling Morag "a slut." The sooner she leaves, the better.

Morag's new landlady, Fan Brady, is very different from Maggie Tefler. She works nights in a club called the Figleaf — a title somewhat misleading, as Morag mutely observes.

Fan is "not yer common-or-garden stripper. . . ." She is a "danseuse" — a lady who takes off her clothes while dancing. It is her work, and she takes it seriously. She exercises, diets, smears perfumed pastel creams all over her body and paints her face weirdly. Her hair is a mass of flaming red ringlets, her face monkey-like, her body tiny and bird-boned, her chest impressive. Fan reminds Morag of the character "Lilac Stonehouse," in *Spear of Innocence*, and she wonders about fiction foreshadowing real life. But Fan is tougher and more cynical than Lilac.

When Morag offers to show Fan her baby, Fan reveals that she has had five abortions and does not take to well to children. When she sees Pique, her first thought is that the father probably is not supporting her. She advises Morag to pressure the father for money. Morag bluntly tells her never to advise her what she should do. Fan is taken aback. Morag says she understands no harm was meant, but repeats her assertion.

Fan then asks Morag advice about changing her nightclub act. Fan, who admits to being almost thirty-four, is about to become a snake-dancer. Morag is somewhat taken aback — particularly when she learns Fan's new partner, a cream and brown python named Tiny, is living in the basement. Although Fan assures her that Tiny is tranquilized, Morag still has visions of Pique being squeezed to death. Morag concludes that her landlady is "nutty as crunchy peanut butter," yet she is beginning to like her.

Memorybank Movie #38, "Travelling On," begins with a snapshot. One-year-old Pique's straight black hair is carefully brushed. Her round face is serious, her big dark eyes look out trustfully at her mother. Fan worries that Morag's whole life revolves around Pique. Morag claims that she also has her work, but Fan thinks Morag needs to meet some men.

Morag admits that she sometimes misses men. Fan, on the other hand, says she has lots of sex, but doesn't like it and often wishes she were lesbian. Morag reflects on the irony: Fan has lots of men and doesn't like them; Morag has no men and misses them. Have they each set things up that way for themselves?

Memorybank Movie #39 features Morag's first man since Jules and is suggestively titled: "Harold, Lover of My What." Morag goes to a party thrown by Hank Masterson where she meets Harold, a slightly drunken newscaster who has just separated from his wife. He and Morag go back to her apartment together. Afterwards, Harold says he'll call her. Morag is unsure, but he does, a few days later. This time they go to Harold's apartment.

Harold drinks a half-bottle of scotch and starts talking about his wife, which bores Morag tremendously. Then, against her wishes, Harold drunkenly drives her home. He takes her hand and weepingly tells her that he loves his wife. After that, he does not call again.

Memorybank Movie #40 is called "Chas" after the single most nasty character in the novel.

The film opens with another snapshot of Pique at about three years of age. She looks like Jules and Morag and like neither. Morag wonders: will Pique later have memories of things this photo doesn't show?

One evening after Pique has fallen asleep, the doorbell rings. It is Chas, one of Fan's "occasional men." This time, he has come to see Morag. Thin, handsome, he is both attractive and repelling. She lets him in, but things get out of hand, and he will not leave when Morag asks him to.

When Chas grabs her, Morag is frightened. She doesn't know his full name, she doesn't really know who he is. All she knows is that she and her daughter are alone in the house with a man who could injure her. What has she got herself into? What if he harms Pique? Words, she knows, will not reach him. They silently struggle for a few seconds, and Morag sees pure acid hatred in his eyes. She considers he may be seeing the same expression in hers. He drops her arm, asks if he scared her and pretends he was joking around. Morag tells him to get out. He agrees — the strikes her across the chest before he leaves.

When Morag recovers, she locks the doors, pours the rest of the rye they had been drinking down the sink, and vomits in the washroom. Then she begins to shake. After checking to see that Pique is safely asleep, she takes a hot bath to calm down. This incident forces Morag to examine her needs and motives. She is especially concerned when she begins to fear she is pregnant. Luckily she is not. She vows she will never again sleep with a man whose child she wouldn't care to bear.

A few weeks later Morag writes to Ella to congratulate her on a publisher's acceptance of a book of her poems. She tells Ella that *her* new work, *Prospero's Child*, is almost through its first draft. She talks about what she is trying to achieve and admits that she is being ambitious. Then she describes Fan and her snake dance. Fan and Tiny put on a private performance for Morag and Pique, and Morag admits that the performance was impressive — oriental music on a record, Fan draped with mauve chiffon, sequins and gold lace, Tiny twisting round his mistress's gyrating body. Pique is quite lacking in fear, and Fan is coming to like her, but Morag is starting to worry about Fan, who is no longer young. Her nerves are shot, and she claims not to think about the future.

According to his letters, Christie is starting to show his age too. Morag writes more often now and sends him money when she can, but she can't go back to Manawaka. She wants to find her own home, but does not know where it could be. Perhaps England — she'd like to go there, even though she might be disappointed. She would also like to go to Scotland, to Sutherland, "where my people came from." She doesn't know what she would learn there, but feels that some day she must go. But not yet — she hasn't enough money and she feels she can't leave Fan right now. Morag concludes her letter by sending her love to Mrs. Gerson and to Ella.

Unsure what else she can do with her novel, Morag submits it. It is accepted by three publishers — Canadian, British and American. As Morag begins the task of revising her book, she becomes determined to do her best. The novel is published, and Hank Masterson throws a party for her. Morag would rather have the party money, but she says nothing.

Memorybank Movie #41 is another which begins with a snapshot of Pique. She is four years old, anxious and proud as she touches Tiny's tail while a frail-looking Fan holds Tiny's head. It is Tiny's first and last photo. One evening, a scream from the basement disturbs the Gunns. Morag finds Fan downstairs crying. Tiny is dead. Fan feels guilty that she had not obeyed her intuition that Tiny was ailing and taken him to a veterinarian. She admits that dancing with Tiny was a gimmick she had adopted to try to stave off her fears of getting old. What will she do now?

Morag cannot answer. She watches the tears cracking the makeup on Fan's face. If you are a "danseuse," you cannot grow old. All Morag can do is fix a stiff rye for Fan. They bury Tiny in the garden; the next day Pique helps make a gravestone for the dead python.

Princess Eureka's dancing days are over. She burns her flimsy costume and gets a job as a coat-check girl. Morag, who has received advance royalties on *Prospero's Child*, insists on helping by paying more rent.

One day, Brooke arrives. He learned from her publishers where she was living, and ". . . just happened to be in Vancouver. . . ." Brooke's second wife, Anne, is slender, immaculately dressed, fashionably coiffured, everything Morag currently is not. Anne and Brooke sit perched on the edge of their chairs as Pique is briefly introduced to them.

Although Brooke may well have had other reasons for bringing his second wife to meet her, Morag sees that he is genuinely concerned for her (Morag's) welfare. However, when Morag starts talking about Fan and her dead snake, Anne's composure is broken and Brooke looks uncomfortable. After fifteen minutes, they depart.

Morag wonders why they came. Was he showing off his wife? But she was showing off her child. It strikes her that they have had to hurt each other one last time.

Memorybank Movie #42, "Songs" opens with a colour photo of five-year-old Pique, round-faced and in a frilly pink dress. Both she and Morag are smiling hesitantly at someone who refuses to have his picture taken.

The "someone" is Jules, who has appeared for the first time in almost six years. He wears his hair in a black mane and his face increasingly resembles the face of Lazarus.

After they embrace, Morag takes Jules upstairs to see Pique while Fan disappears into her own room. Jules seems disappointed when he hears that Morag cannot bear to call his daughter Piquette, but he seeks no explanation. Morag says that she has told Pique that her father could not be around because he has to travel and sing songs for people.

Jules and Pique approach each other warily. Pique knows who he is, but is guarded in her response to him. Jules asks Morag for a drink, then pulls out some photos. Pique recognizes the one of her at two months. Jules shows her where he has written her name on the back. He spells out to her that he is indeed her dad. Piquette is quiet, getting used to the presence of the father she has never seen before. Later she bids him goodnight, but calls him no name.

Jules stays with Morag and Pique for some months. He has come to see his sister, Val, who is sick. Morag did not know she was in Vancouver. When she offers any help to her she can give, Jules brusquely tells her she could not help in any way, and he will not let her forget that.

His brother Jacques has settled near Galloping Mountain. Unlike Lazarus and Jules, he is a solid, steady man. The youngest brother, Paul, was drowned up north, where he was acting as a guide for American tourists. Jules does not believe the story that he was drowned, since Paul was an expert canoeist. Jacques had sought an enquiry into his disappearance, but the authorities took the word of the Americans. Only Jacques and Jules are left; Val won't live much longer. Morag knows there is nothing she can say.

Jules is out most days. Morag does not question him, but he tells her first that Val is in hospital and then, later, that she has left. Sometimes he comes home drunk, but only after Pique is asleep. Most often he is silent when his depressions hit.

He and Pique come to like each other. She tries to impress him and he teases her. At first, she will not call him Dad, but, because he wants her to, she later does. Then it is Dad, Dad, Dad, all the time.

One evening Jules gets out his guitar. He and Billy Joe are still a team, playing to people across the country. The younger kids in coffeehouses are more responsive than their elders to the original songs of the duo, but Billy Joe and Jules are starting to feel more competition from the new generation of folksingers of the early sixties.

Jules sings his song of Old Jules, his grandfather, for Morag and Pique. Pique likes the strong, simple lyrics and the tune; Morag is moved to tears by the echoes and all the things Jules puts into song that he could not put into talk. The song deals with the eighteen-year-old Jules during the North-West Rebellion of 1885: "His heart is true, his heart is strong,/ He knows the land where his people belong." It ends with the lines: "They say the dead don't always die;/ They say the truth outlives the lie —/ The night wind calls their voices there,/ The Métis men, like Jules Tonnerre."

When Jules tells Pique that the song is about her great-grandfather, the word and the concept are foreign to Pique. She cannot comprehend a time so long ago. She asks her father to sing the song again, but he says, "Someday." He sings some other songs. Pique wants a song for herself. Jules again says, "Someday." Perhaps someday Pique will write a song for him, he suggests. Pique doesn't know.

One night he tells Morag it's time for him to travel on. He does not say goodbye to Pique. When Pique learns her father is gone, she asks no questions. Morag wonders what effect this sudden appearance and disappearance of a father will have on Pique's later life.

One day Fan announces that she has lost her job. She will go back to the Okanagan Valley where her sister lives. Morag also decides to make some changes in her life. She will travel to England and Scotland. For some time she has known that she must, but now the time has come. When Fan and Morag go their separate ways, they promise to keep in touch, knowing they won't. They do know, however, that they won't forget each other.

Commentary

The section set in the continuing present which opens Chapter 8 is short but significant. Morag is still fascinated by the paradoxical double flow of the river, even though she has lived beside it for some time now. Nature, time and the river do not lose their power to enthrall her any more than do human nature, time and memory. The parallels and the paradoxes are all there.

The reference to the trees as "ancestors, carrying within them the land's past" (p. 285) is interesting. Morag implies her growing identification with the land, with Canada — her "home and native land." The whole of Part Four is so much concerned with the theme of home, of land and one's relationship to one's roots in the land. The willows and maples are solidly rooted here by the river where Morag has chosen to plant herself and create her own home.

The theme of ancestors is picked up later with the references to Catharine Parr Traill, the hard-working, controlled, orderly ancestor Morag has adopted. The continuity through past, present, and future reaches its logical culmination in the last paragraph of the opening section with Morag's reference to Pique, the future, as "harbinger of my death, continuer of life."

The second paragraph of the chapter refers to "the kids" — young Pique and her new lover Dan who have moved into Morag's house. To Morag they reverse the "order of life" with their living at night and sleeping through the day, just as the wind reverses the flow of the river established by its natural current. Order flows in Morag's blood, she acknowledges, despise it as she may. But it is *her* sense of order, born of *her* nature, and not to be confused with Nature's order — whatever that might be.

Morag herself is trying to adjust throughout this summer to the flow of her life, and to her own aging. At forty-seven she is going through other "Rites of Passage" — an initiation into a new maturity of middle age. Similarly, the sections contained within the memorybank movies in Part Four deal with her coming to terms with herself after leaving Brooke and being his "little one." We are reminded that living is a process, that growth continues until the silence of death and that we are constantly discovering who and where we are.

One of the main things Morag is brought to accept in this section is the paradox that she is, as her daughter puts it, alone and yet not alone. Through the help of the young (Pique and Dan) and the old (Royland), Morag comes to swallow her pride and her guilt. She envies the young and she envies Mrs. Traill. Still, she is learning to accept middle age.

The reference to ancestors (and to Mrs. Traill) and their continued influence on Morag's present is picked up by Jules' references in his song at the end of the chapter. There he sings of his adopted ancestor, Louis Riel. "They say the dead don't always die," he sings, and his song is proof of that.

Morag wonders then, as does Jules, if Pique will grow up to sing of her father. And, wonders Morag, "How will the tales change in the telling?" We are constantly recalling and revising the past, which is then passed on as a gift to the future.

Morag's letter to Dan McRaith, her former lover in Scotland, is another reminder of the continuance of the past in her personal present. Even though she and Dan are now separated in space and time, they are still close.

When she refers to the continuing importance of names to her, we might note the meaning of her name. "Gunn" comes from the ancient Norse word "gunnr" which means "war." Thus her statement that she is "still fighting the same bloody battles as always, inside the skull" is a subtle suggestion that our names are intimately indicative of our identity.

The theme of home in this chapter deserves a few other comments. Morag, in her forties, has established her home by the river back in Canada. In Vancouver, she wonders where home might be. She writes Ella that she needs to find a home, a real home. The "Bleak House" of the first memorybank movie is not home.

Still, Vancouver is a stage in her transition to find herself and her place. Becoming a single mother, a writer and a person calls upon all of Morag's faith and determination. But she is a survivor, and she learns to cope with the responsibilities, uncertainties, doubts, challenges and people she meets.

Certainly the people she meets are fascinating. Martyred Mrs. Maggie Tefler, exotic Fan Brady, nasty Chas, sad Harold, and the child Pique engage the reader's imagination as well as Morag's. In fact, Morag often wonders if fiction can ever really outdo real life in its strangeness and seeming incredibility.

Several semi-parallels between Morag and Pique are made in this chapter. Snapshots precede memorybank movies. This time the snaps are of Pique; in Chapter 1 they were of Morag. Morag's storytelling is echoed by Pique's telling stories to her mother. And Pique's questions, beginning "What means ——?" echo Morag's. They are similar yet unique, this mother and daughter.

Morag's long letter to Ella deserves comment. Morag writes of the second novel she is working on — *Prospero's Child*. It echoes both Shakespeare's *The Tempest* and Morag's marriage to Brooke, but, because it is her creation it is different from both. In the play, Prospero's child is his daughter, Miranda; in the marriage, Morag was Brooke-Prospero's "little one." In Morag's novel, the child-wife must reject the "prince" she formerly worshipped "in order to become her own person." So the theme of freedom is vital in all three cases. At the end of the Shakespearian play, *The Tempest*, Prospero breaks his magic wand, abandons his powers gracefully, and releases the inhabitants of his enchanted isle to find their own freedom. In the Skelton marriage, Morag releases herself with the aid of her shaman, Jules, through sexual union.

Morag wonders to Ella if she, like Prospero of the play, could willingly surrender her creative powers as he did. She admires Prospero's statement: "What strength I have's mine own, Which is most faint —" and wonders if she could hang onto that knowledge which is true strength. She admires his recognition that "his real enemy is despair within, and that he stands in need of grace, like everyone else." This is a foreshadowing of the end of *The Diviners*. Morag is here recognizing both her affinity with the human community and the enemy within herself, rather than blaming perceived enemies without.

The chapter ends with Morag leaving once more, this time going east from Vancouver to the old world — to England and to Scotland where she will live and continue her rites of passage.

Notes

Limoges: French city famous for its fine porcelain china-ware. (p. 287)

teleport: To move one's body through space and time. (p. 288)

Presbyterian: Member of the Church of Scotland. Presbyterians traditionally have a strong sense of the sinfullness of mankind. (p. 290)

harbinger: A herald or forerunner signifying something to come. (p. 290)

Bleak House: This Memorybank Movie title refers to Morag's first boardinghouse in Vancouver. It alludes to the grim novel by Charles Dickens of the same title. (p. 290)

Kitsilano: Neighbourhood in the west part of Vancouver, fronting on the sea. (p. 291)

a bun in the oven: Slang phrase for being pregnant. (p. 292)

preggers: Slang word for pregnant. (p. 292)

alkie: Slang word for alcoholic. (p. 292)

Virginia Woolf: Renowned English novelist and essayist (1882-1941). Her long essay *A Room of One's Own* defines the need for privacy if a woman is to write. (pp. 293-294)

You Can't Go Home Again: Sprawling epic novel by the American writer Thomas Wolfe (1900-1938). The title spells out one of his novel's main themes: once out on his own, the artist must keep on going, further and further away from his roots. Morag, on the other hand, believes that "you have to go home again, in some way or other." (p. 302)

North Van: The city of North Vancouver, across Burrard Inlet from Vancouver. (p. 302)

Seconal: Brand-name tranquilizer. (p. 309)

danseuse: The French word for a female dancer — usually a stripper. In English, the word is considered pretentious. (p. 309)

clipjoint: A club or restaurant which "clips" or overcharges customers. (p. 309)

the Okanagan: The Okanagan Valley in the southern interior of British Columbia is a prime fruit-growing area. (p. 314)

lez: Slang for lesbian. (p. 317)

Kama Sutra: Classic Sanskrit (Ancient Indian) book on love and sex. (p. 318)

Qu'Appelle: The Qu'Appelle Valley in what is now east-central Saskatchewan was where the Métis, dispossessed of their lands in the Red River Valley, settled after Manitoba became a province in 1870. (p. 344)

Macdonald: Sir John A. Macdonald, Prime Minister of Canada (1867-1873 and 1878-1891). Macdonald ordered troops to put down the Red River Rebellion of 1869-1870 and the North-West Rebellion of 1885. When Louis Riel was sentenced to hang for treason in 1885 in Regina, Macdonald refused to commute the sentence and thus earned the undying hatred of French-Canadians. (p. 345)

"The Yellow Rose of Texas": Popular American song from the film *Battle Cry*, recorded by Mitch Miller in 1955. A country and western ballad with a military beat, to Jules it symbolizes the imported American pop culture which his generation prefers to Canadian folk songs such as his own. (p. 346)

Ojibway: Amerindian tribe of Northern Ontario. Like the Cree, Ojibways speak a dialect of Algonkian. (p. 346)

CHAPTER 9

Summary

Morag is sitting in the kitchen, attempting to work, when Pique interrupts her. Her daughter observes that Morag seems to be putting down words, and Morag, who does not like to talk about what she is doing, turns the topic to Pique's newly braided hair.

Pique remarks that it is cooler to have braids and — anyhow — she is part-Indian. She no longer wants to live a split life; she really wants to know where she belongs. When her mother questions if it is an either/or situation, Pique angrily asserts that Morag could not know what it is like. Besides, Morag has always brought up Pique in *her* way of life, and Pique feels she has never got much of the Indian side.

Morag is hurt. Pique declares that she has never known "what really happened." She remembers the one time her father had been with them; she remembers his songs and the things he told her when she saw him in Toronto.

But what of the stories Morag told Pique when she was young? Morag says that some of them were true stories and some were not, and it doesn't matter. To Pique it *does* matter. "I want to know what really happened," she repeats. Morag's reply that there is no one authentic version fails to satisfy Pique. But she apologizes to her mother and admits that her attitude relates to what is bothering her.

Pique is not pleased by Dan and A-Okay's plans to raise horses. Dan is going to quit his job to work with the horses, leaving Pique to bring in the money. She is not thrilled by the idea of working as a supermarket cashier in order to finance the dreams of Dan and A-Okay. She has told Dan of her misgivings. He has promised that as soon as the horse-breeding starts bringing in money, she can work on the farm. Pique, however, has plans to travel out West again.

When Dan comes over later that afternoon to talk, Morag puts away her writing and curses silently. She cares for them all, but when can she do her work?

Dan questions her about why Pique would want to go out West. Morag doesn't know, but feels that perhaps Pique has a deep need to find her "family." In the discussion that follows, Dan reveals that although he is rebelling from the way his father lives, certain elements of (Dan's) own lifestyle are quite similar. He defensively proclaims that he must make his *own* kind of place. Morag agrees: it will be different and yet, in some ways, the same. Dan insists that it will be different if he can help it, but Morag suggests that it is not within his will. "You can change a whole lot. But you can't throw him away entirely. He and a lot of others are there. Here," and she touches the vein on Dan's wrist. Although she knows she has touched a responsive nerve in Dan, Morag realizes it will take time for him to recognize the truth of her words.

That evening, out on the cool river with Royland, Morag thinks she can survive the heat of the summer and looks forward to the brief respite of autumn, before the harsh Canadian winter sets in. As she gazes upon the land sweeping down to the riverbanks, Morag thinks it ironic that she, who hates cities and who has come to live in the country, still does not swim in the river because of her fear of the weeds. In New York City, she reflects, her agent's fears are proclaimed by three locks on the apartment door.

Even so, Morag muses, perhaps she should have raised her child in cities, where she would have learned the practical techniques for surviving in a world dedicated to "Death, Slavery, and the Pursuit of Unhappiness." Instead, she has retreated, figuratively, to an island.

These meditations are broken by Royland's sudden command to turn off the boat's motor. A Great Blue Heron, once common but now a rare sight, is probing the shallows of the river for fish. When it spots the boat, it gracefully glides away. Royland reels in his line and silently, awestruck, he and Morag go home.

"Sceptr'd Isle" is the title of Memorybank Movie #43, into which Morag's musings on islands have led her. Here Morag and Pique are literally on an island — they are living in England, and suffering through a particularly grim British winter. The thick smog which fills the air terrifies Morag, but Pique loves it. One foggy day, a greengrocer asks Morag what she thinks of "this royal throne of kings, this sceptr'd isle," and Morag is surprised to find a working man who can quote Shakespeare.

Morag has found a basement flat on Hedgerow Walk in Hampstead, London. In spite of what the address implies, it is not a romantic, rural setting. Nevertheless, Morag is not afraid of living in the city of London. The myth that the English are a law-abiding, orderly people still persists in her mind. Morag likes England and feels quite at home in her new country. She realizes, however, that she will never truly belong.

One of the reasons Morag came to England was a fantasy about mingling with fellow-writers as friends. She has friends, but few are writers, and she finds that London can be just as provincial as Canada. She and Pique have established a kind of refuge in London. The idea of moving again does not appeal to either of them.

Morag works part-time at a bookstore owned by Mr. Sampson. He calls it Agonistes Bookshop, an allusion to the poem by John Milton about the Biblical hero, Samson Agonistes. Mr. Sampson says he is doing his best against the philistines, or small-minded people, through his love of books. Despite his insistence that one "must be ruthless to survive," he often lets poor students read through entire books in his store, without pressing for a sale. Also he is sympathetic to Morag's need to look after Pique — and to write.

When Pique becomes ill Morag must stay home and care for her. She relates to Pique the tales of Piper Gunn and of Lazarus Tonnerre. She tells her daughter about Christie and how she used to believe every word of the tales Christie told her. Later, she came to disbelieve him and, finally, she was able to realize that the stories were based on events that occurred, but nobody could tell what *really* happened. "So I started believing in them again, in a different way," she says.

During this time of caring for Pique, Morag cannot write and, because she has no one to talk with and assure her that all will be well, she feels very alone. She also worries about losing her job. Mr. Sampson is understanding and sympathetic, but he needs his assistant. When Morag finally is able to return to the shop, she finds Mr. Sampson in a panic over his accounts. She agrees to work full days for the next two weeks to help him out. This will mean that one month will have passed with no writing accomplished. Morag knows how difficult it will be to resume work on her novel.

When a letter arrives from Christie, asking when Morag plans to travel to Sutherland, the home county of her ancestors, Morag wonders why her pilgrimage has been so long delayed. Perhaps she is afraid of being disillusioned or that she will not learn or understand anything more about her past. Perhaps she will feel too much and understand too much. Then she remembers what Christie had told her about the Gunns being cast on the shores of Sutherland and dispossessed of their homes. She writes to Christie, assuring him that she will go on her pilgrimage soon.

One afternoon in the bookshop Morag notices a man who has been looking through a book for an hour. She does not find him particularly handsome, but she is attracted to him. She discovers that his name is Dan McRaith. He is a painter from the Highland village of Crombruach, in Scotland. As they chat, Morag observes that her people lost their Gaelic tongue, and McRaith replies that the same is true of most present-day Scots. This man reminds Morag of Christie: she feels an echo of the lost Gaelic in their voices. Although Dan McRaith is married and has children, Morag decides that this does not matter. She arranges to meet him in a pub that same evening.

Morag and Dan are able to talk openly with one another. He is 45 and has been married to Bridie for 25 years. They have seven children. He doesn't complain about her preoccupation with children; she does not complain about his with painting. Soon, Morag is talking about herself, telling Dan about Brooke and Christie and her life in Manawaka. She finds it incredible that she can talk to him so easily. It does not seem strange that later, after the pub, they spend the night together.

Almost two months pass, and Morag is still seeing Dan. When he has to get away from his home village, he takes a room at a friend's house in Camden Town. His paints are always put away when Morag visits and he does not let her see what he is working on.

Juggling her job, her time with Dan and evenings with Pique interferes greatly with Morag's writing. One afternoon she is annoyed to be interrupted in her work on her novel by a phone call from Dan. Morag had lost track of the time. She tells Dan that this will happen sometimes and that there is nothing to be done about it. Dan apologizes, assuring her that he respects her for standing up to him, which is something his wife never does. He observes that neither has seen the other working. McRaith admits that he has borrowed two of Morag's books from the library. He finds it strange that her characters "could be you and yet not you, at the same time." Morag is pleased by his understanding. He then offers to show her some of his paintings, which he has brought down from Scotland to sell in London. Once he has finished a painting, he feels no pain in selling it. Morag admits that she never reads one of her books when it is published. Each of them is detached from the work once it is delivered into the world.

Dan wonders aloud if Morag will ever base a character in one of her novels on him. She does not think she has the right. She gives him the right to paint her, though, if he so wishes. The painting Dan does of Morag is the only one he completes in London and does not destroy. He depicts Morag's face in shadow, framed by her black hair. But it is the eyes which are most striking — and unmistakably Morag's.

Memorybank Movie #44 is called "The Black Isle." The title refers to that part of Ross-shire in the Scottish Highlands where McRaith's village of Crombruach is located.

Morag has known Dan McRaith for three years now and sees him for a few weeks or months twice a year, when he comes to London. She is increasingly resentful about this but never tells McRaith.

One evening Dan phones her to announce that he is going home and wants her to come over right away. Morag tells her daughter she is going over to see Dan McRaith — a friend who is having a get-together before going home to Scotland. She wonders if Pique suspects she is having an affair with Dan, but she cannot tell her daughter she is having a relationship with a married man.

Dan is in his room, nervously pacing the floor. As he pours whiskey for them, he is shaking. Morag does not understand why he has to go, but she knows he must. Dan suggests that if Morag were to visit Crombruach, she would perhaps understand where he is coming from. She could stay at the local inn, and, if she wanted to, he could drive her up to Sutherland, home of her ancestors. Bridie would not suspect anything amiss if Morag were to arrive with Pique. Morag doubts this and says she could not possibly visit Crombruach. However, when Dan leaves, she misses him. A month later, she writes to say that she is coming north after all.

On the train to Inverness, Morag is concerned that she is making a mistake. Quite simply, she is motivated by curiosity to see Crombruach and Bridie so she can understand why Dan keeps going back home. Also, she did promise Christie that she would make a pilgrimage to Sutherland: this is an opportunity to do so.

Morag and Pique are met at the Inverness train station by Dan. After dropping off their suitcases at the village inn, the three drive to the McRaith cottage. Bridie comes down the stairs with two of the children. She and Morag regard one another warily.

Bridie is about forty-five, but looks older than Dan. A handsome, slight woman with a sharp-featured face, she wears sensible shoes and a brown sweater and skirt. Morag realizes that Bridie is no longer a fantasy woman: she is real, she is here, and she stands between Morag and Dan. When Bridie apologizes for not having much to offer her husband's London friends, Morag realizes that Bridie is not suspicious of her at all. She is just shy — and perhaps a bit resentful of those who come from what is to her another world.

Morag and Pique stay in Crombruach for five days: Pique

enjoys the company of the other children, while Morag takes long walks with Dan in the countryside and along the seashore. The idea of the pilgrimage to Sutherland is abandoned. After considering, Morag realizes that she doesn't really want to go. By way of explanation, she remarks, "It has to do with Christie. The myths are my reality." Morag sees now that Scotland is not her land. What she thought of for so long as the home of her ancestors is no longer that for her. Her country is "Christie's real country. Where I was born."

Morag also understands the extent to which Dan and Bridie belong to Crombruach. It is their home — their place. The time comes to leave. Morag and Dan say farewell in Inverness. Their affair has come to an end.

Two months later, a telegram arrives from Dr. Cates in Manawaka with the news that Christie is very ill. Morag announces to her daughter that they are going "home." Pique does not know the meaning of "home," but now Morag realizes that it is Canada.

"The Ridge of Tears" is the war cry of the Logan clan and it is, appropriately, the title of Memorybank Movie #45, which deals with Morag's return to Manawaka for the death of Christie.

Pique is left in Winnipeg with Mrs. Gerson so that Morag can travel to Manawaka alone. When she arrives at the hospital, Morag asks the receptionist for Christie Logan, her stepfather. The receptionist recognizes that the woman must be Morag Gunn and shyly tells her that she has read her books and that Manawaka is proud of her.

The nurse warns Morag that Christie can only mumble garbled words now. Under the sheets, he seems shrunken, a mere skeleton. Morag speaks to him, and his eyes open. Strangely, they are the clear blue of years ago. As Morag apologizes for not having come before, Christie strains to speak but cannot. She sees the agony in his eyes, sees his shame as he turns his head from her, and feels he must sense himself somehow diminished in her eyes.

As they sit together silently, with clasped hands, Morag feels the blood coursing through his veins. A breezy young nurse enters, carrying a bedpan. Christie tries to push her away, uttering a sound like a growl and a sob. Morag turns on the nurse angrily and tells her to get out. Then Morag returns her gaze to Christie and sees that he has recovered: his eyes are shrewd and mocking, his mouth shaping a soundless laugh. Morag laughs too — a defensive measure she and Christie have always shared.

Before leaving the hospital, there is something Morag hopes she can find the words to say: "Christie — I used to fight a lot with you, Christie, but you've been my father to me," she confesses. She can just make out his whispered reply and, gazing into his eyes, Morag can see that the words have been chosen carefully: "Well — I'm blessed."

Morag sleeps in her old room on Hill Street that night. It is the first time she has ever slept here alone. No ghosts disturb her, but the spirits of Prin, Piper Gunn, Clowny Macpherson and many other characters, both real and fictional, combine and commune in her head. She is woken in the morning by Mrs. Winkler, calling from downstairs. The hospital wants Morag to go there right away. When Morag reaches the hospital, Christie is dead.

It is up to Morag to make the funeral arrangements. At the Japonica Chapel she meets with Hector Jones, the funeral director. He says that he feels that he knows her already. He has read her books and greets her as a local girl. He did not know Christie, he admits. Morag says that no one really did, even though he lived in Manawaka all his life. Hector asks why that would be so, and Morag says it was because Christie was the town scavenger and a bit of a maverick. Hector offers her a drink. She is struck by his public relations veneer, but sees a genuine, kind person behind the surface.

Morag insists that Christie be buried beside Prin in the Manawaka Cemetery under a grey granite stone. Then she asks that arrangements be made for a piper to play at Christie's burial. Hector sighs, but agrees to ask old Scotty Grant if he will oblige. The scene ends in crazy laughter after she thanks Hector and he says, "Any time." They both recognize the absurdity of the statement.

On the day of the funeral, the young minister from the United Church reads the service at Christie's grave. Morag and Hector stand by. Scotty Grant, casually dressed, asks Morag if she is sure she wants to go through with it. She says "yes", and adds, "please."

Scotty Grant begins to play "The Flowers of the Forest,"

the ancient lament for the dead. And Morag sees, "with the strength of conviction, that this is Christie's true burial." As she thinks of Piper Gunn, the giant with the strength of conviction of whom Christie had told her stories so long ago, Morag is "released into her mourning."

Commentary

Morag's life by the river, working at her writing, is interrupted constantly. Paradoxically, she reflects that the only thing worse than being interrupted is *not* being interrupted.

We are reminded that, throughout the continuing present of *The Diviners*, Margaret Laurence has Morag Gunn trying to write a novel. We never find out precisely what Morag is writing *about*, but several critics have suggested that the memorybank movies which play through Morag's head are the basis, or even the content, of the novel she is writing. Certainly Morag reminds us several times that we are constantly recalling and revising the past and that fact and fiction, memory and invention interweave. The phrase from Chapter 8 — "How will the tales change in the telling?" — must echo in our minds.

Pique interrupts Morag's writing to announce that she is tired of being half-white and half-Métis — which is in itself a blend of two races. She seeks identity, integrity and a sense of belonging. Pique, who is still in her rebellious stage, needs to find who she is and where she fits in. She needs "a place to stand on." Morag, who is now more reconciled, more adjusted, has found her place; but Pique has not.

Pique's complaint that she never knew what really happened, an echo of Morag's earlier complaints to Christie, brings from Morag an echo of Christie. Her rejoinder to Pique's wondering if the stories of her past "happened like that or not" is almost in Christie's language: "Some did and some didn't, I guess. It doesn't matter a damn. Don't you see?"

Pique doesn't see. "I want to know what really happened," she insists. Morag's "Well, so do I" is an admission that she is still searching, still divining. "But there is no one version. There just isn't." This is the distilled wisdom of her life, and perhaps one of the simplest and most profound truths which emerges from *The Diviners*. Pique does not agree, but she relents. "Maybe not," she admits. She will have to make the discovery herself. The truths of our mothers and fathers have to be found out *by* ourselves *for* ourselves before they are genuinely truths for us.

Pique must create her own meaning, her own identity and her own home. It's not her mother's, nor is it necessarily a farm with Dan. She will have to go out West and search there. Conversely, Dan is searching for the same things, but he has left the West and his father's horse ranch in Alberta to come East. This is an echo of Morag's own experience. She tells Dan, out of the wisdom gained through her experience, that she realized that "the whole town was inside my head, for as long as I live". This is itself an echo of Christie's advice about Manawaka: "It'll all go with you." Now she realizes the inner truth he had communicated to her when she was too young and inexperienced to recognize its wisdom. The past flows in our blood, she advises Dan, touching the vein along his wrist.

The episode which concludes the section of Chapter 9, dealing with Morag in the continuing present, demands special attention. It is what is known in literature as an *epiphany*. This is a revelation, an event in which an inner truth or essential reality is suddenly perceived. Usually this intuitive recognition comes without warning, like a flash of lightning. Something — often (though not necessarily) commonplace — is seen in a new light as something rich and strange. Afterwards, we can never be quite the same again.

It is evening, and Morag is out with Royland in his boat on the river. Royland glimpses the rare and beautiful Great Blue Heron. They watch, "in silence, in awe," as the single bird takes flight and sweeps gracefully through the air "like something out of the world's dawn." A representative of a once-populous, now near-extinct species, fragile-seeming yet strong, the heron may suggest to us our place on this planet as an endangered species, "speeding not only towards individual death, but probably the death of its kind."

The power of this passage comes through in the poetic prose Laurence so eloquently employs and through its singular suggestiveness. Laurence is, perhaps, at her best when she is *not* explicitly making a statement, when she allows the reader to recognize in a flash that, as the philosopher Ludwig Wittgenstein wrote, "Whereof one cannot speak, one must be silent."

Morag is silent. But that evening she recognizes that she is not isolated, not on an island, not questing anymore for an individual solitude. Her searching has brought her to where she is now — to a human community in her native land.

The memorybank movie "Sceptr'd Isle" shows Morag living in England. Working, writing, mothering — and fluctuating, "like a pendulum," — she is constantly in motion. She tells stories to Pique and finds herself making Christie into a mythical figure. Meanwhile, she succeeds in ignoring the real living Christie in Manawaka, writing him only the occasional letter. Pique never meets Christie; she only knows the recalled and revised Christie who lives in Morag's tales, just as Morag only knew Piper and Morag Gunn through Christie's tales.

Of these earlier stories, Morag tells Pique that she used to take them at face value, believing every word. Then, impressed by "fact" and "what really happened," she came to disbelieve them entirely. Her later recognition that the tales were based on facts paralleled her own growing realization of herself as a teller of tales. When she came to wonder if one could ever know what really happened, she "started believing in them again, in a different way." Thus she moves from naive literal acceptance, through scepticism and agnosticism, to a new and different understanding and acceptance of essential inner truths. This foreshadows Morag's recognition in Scotland that "The myths are my reality." Myth blends fact and fiction, history and memory, the personal and the universal.

Morag also tells Pique about "strength of conviction," which characteristic was exemplified by Piper and his Morag. She explains that it means faith and that one must have it to survive. She is a teacher, and, despite what some might think of her swearing and her occasional sex life, an intensely moral person.

When Morag tells Pique stories she recalls from Jules about his father and his people, she is trying to give her daughter a sense of her complex heritage. Pique's determination to go to Galloping Mountain foreshadows her journey there in the novel's concluding chapter.

Morag's meeting with Dan McRaith in England, and her spiritual and sexual connection with him, is important. With him, she is with a fellow artist and fellow pilgrim. Like Ella and like Jules, he will be her friend for life — another reassurance that "no man is an Island, entire of himself."

Sometimes, in order to gain a new perspective on a particular situation, it is necessary to travel — to distance oneself.

So it is with Morag's visit to Scotland. There she realizes that she and Dan cannot be long-term lovers. He is bound to his wife and family and place, even though he must periodically leave them. There, too, overlooking the firth to Sutherland, she is struck by the sudden realization that Scotland is Dan's place, but her place is in Canada. When, after returning to London, she learns that Christie is dying, she tells Pique that they are going home. Home has no real meaning for Pique yet, but for Morag it means *Canada*, Christie's country.

Canada is the land of her fathers. When she greets Christie on his death bed, she can finally tell him, from the heart, her realization that he was a father to her. This understanding frees her and marks an essential rite of passage in Morag's long pilgrimage to find who she is and where she is coming from. She can claim her heritage as an inheritor and prepare to create her own place in her homeland.

Christie is "blessed" by Morag's simple yet profound acknowledgement of her debt to him, and he dies in peace.

The chapter ends with Morag's giving Christie the funeral he wanted, with a piper playing a lament for the dead over his grave. Morag, listening to the mournful wail of the pipes, sees "with the strength of conviction" that this rite of passage is Christie's "true burial." She is released into her mourning, free at last, another rite of passage completed. And so the chapter concludes with another leave-taking.

Notes

Grendel: The monster dragon in the Anglo-Saxon epic *Beowulf*. (p. 356)

"dedicated to Death, Slavery, and the Pursuit of Unhappiness": Morag's ironic reversal of the American Dream which has now, she perceives, become the World Nightmare. In the opening of the American Declaration of Independence (1776), Thomas Jefferson wrote that men are endowed by God with "certain unalienable rights, among these being Life, Liberty, and the Pursuit of Happiness." (p. 356)

pterodactyl: A member of the extinct prehistoric family of flying reptiles. (p. 357)

Sceptr'd Isle: The Sceptr'd Isle refers to England. The phrase is from John of Gaunt's patriotic speech in Shakespeare's

Richard II. (Act I, scene i, line 40) A sceptre is a rod which symbolizes the divine right of the king to rule as God's steward on earth. "Island" alludes to John Donne's famous Devotion XVII: "No man is an island, entire of itself; every man is a part of the continent, a part of the main." (p. 357)

the Underground: The London subway. (p. 357)

parochial: Restricted to a parish; restricted to a small and narrow world. (p. 359)

Samson Agonistes: Immensely strong, he is the blinded hero of John Milton's long poem of the same name. Samson brings down the temple of the Philistines (ancient inhabitants of Palestine), killing them and himself in the process. "Agonistes" means "one who struggles." (p. 360)

philistine: Now refers to a small-minded, middle-class person who smugly and ignorantly has no time for the arts and culture. (p. 360)

Lansbury's: English publishing house. (p. 360)

out of whole cloth: Out of one's head; a purely made-up story. (p. 367)

strength of conviction: Faith. (pp. 367-368)

croft: A small tenant farm, particularly in the Scottish Highlands. A crofter is a tenant farmer. (p. 370)

Guinness: Brand name of the world-famous Irish stout. Stout is a very dark strong ale. (p. 376)

Dhu: One of several Gaelic words for black. Dan calls Morag "Morag Dhu." (p. 376)

the dispossessed: Those who have been deprived or robbed of their land or identity. (p. 378)

The Black Isle: A part of the Scottish Highlands county of Ross-shire on the Cromarty Firth. (p. 379)

Inverness: City in the Scottish Highlands and terminus of the main railway line from London. (p. 383)

burn: Scottish word for a small brown-coloured creek. (p. 384)

firth: Scottish name for a long, narrow inlet of the sea. (p. 384)

CHAPTER 10

Summary

Along the river, the leaves on the trees are turning red and gold. Morag has been writing all day, but by evening she has writer's cramp, so she walks down to the river to relieve the tension. The swallows, which the day before were everywhere, have responded to the change of season and departed for the south.

When she returns to the house, she leafs through some new books about weeds and wildflowers. Summoning up the spirit of Catharine Parr Traill, Morag engages in an imaginary conversation with that lady, concerning the dangers of poisonous plants. This conversation, Morag vows, will be the last one she will have with Mrs. Traill: "One thing I'm going to stop doing, though," Morag says, is to "stop feeling guilty that I'll never be as hardworking or knowledgeable or all-round terrific as you were." She decides to stop comparing herself unfavourably with Maudie, A-Okay and Pique. She is somewhere in between these old and new pioneers and is not going to worry about it anymore. She recognizes also that she has worked hard, and although she hasn't done all she has wanted to do, she hasn't "folded up like a paper fan, either." With this, Morag bids "farewell, sweet saint," and dismisses the spirit of the pioneer lady forever.

The evening is spent in the company of Pique, Maudie, A-Okay, Tom and Dan. Dan and Pique argue over the fact that Dan has bought a horse. Dan defends his choice of a palomino gelding (which, Morag can't help but point out, is not a breeding horse), while Pique declares that she doesn't understand horses. Morag silently reflects on the irony of Pique, a descendent of one of the prairie horselords, not being interested in horses.

A-Okay tries to restore peace, then turns to Morag. Royland has suggested that, if he and Dan want to get into farming, they could hire themselves out to Charlie Greenhouse, who is preparing to retire, and learn about farming from him. Then they could save enough money to buy the farm they are now renting. Pique, who is not included in these plans, picks up her guitar and starts to sing Jules' song for Lazarus. She is crying as she sings.

The next day, after a poor night's sleep, Morag goes outside into the chilly morning air. Winter will soon set in. Overhead the Canada geese are flying south.

Memorybank Movie #46, "Beulah Land," places Morag in Toronto after leaving Manawaka and Christie's funeral. She is staying with Ella and her second husband, Mort. The book reviews for *Jonah* are generally good, but Morag is as apathetic about them as she is about the sale of it to a book club. The news that *Spear of Innocence* and *Prospero's Child* are coming out in paperback and that a film company has bought an option on *Spear* does not excite her either.

A month passes during which Morag and Pique stay with Ella and Mort. Ella has twin babies and really doesn't need extra company, but she is kind to her friend and insists that Morag has not overstayed her welcome. Nonetheless, Morag apologizes to her for being a bother.

Morag finds that she is bored and depressed. She sleeps to escape the tedium of everyday life. She is avoiding decisions — such as where Pique is going to school in the fall. One day she is lifted out of her gloom by an advertisement in the paper that describes an 80-acre farm for sale near Peterborough, Ontario. It includes a partially-refurbished old farmhouse built by pioneers in the late nineteenth century. Morag decides to view the property — and ends up bringing back a document of intent to purchase the farm. At last she has land. And, she feels, now she has ancestors. She will be a new pioneer, setting down her roots in Ontario.

The Innerfilm which follows takes us inside Morag's mind. She is imagining living in the farmhouse, snug and warm while a blizzard rages outside. Life has fallen into place exactly as she wished. In Morag's fantasy, she has almost finished her latest and best novel. Pique is working on embroidery or rather making a miniature log house. There is plenty of wood for the winter; the basement is filled with preserves Morag has made; the bank account is healthy; and there is a friendly widower next door who is well-read and good-looking.

Memorybank Movie #47 is called "McConnell's Landing." Pique and Morag move into their new house on the river in October. The house needs more work than Morag had realized and the barn is falling down. There are problems with the furnace and the well-pump, and Morag worries about winter setting in. However, when Morag and Pique walk down to the river and see the flaming scarlet maples and the ripples on the river, Morag decides aloud that everything *is* going to be all right. Pique agrees.

An old man with a neat grey beard approaches and introduces

himself as Royland, a neighbour who lives farther down the river. He reveals that his business is finding wells — he is a diviner — and asks Pique if she wants to accompany him on his divining expedition the next day.

Memorybank Movie #48 has the same title as Morag's fourth novel: *Shadow of Eden*. Three years have passed. Morag's novel is finished and has been accepted for publication. Morag is relieved, but feels the usual emptiness that strikes her after a book is finished. Since money is getting low again, she decides to write to Ella rather than phone her. She tells her all about the novel she has just finished and invites Ella and the family to visit her one weekend.

Memorybank Movie #49 is called "Gainsay Who Dare." Pique is now fifteen and asserting her growing independence. Morag is having trouble adjusting to the fact that her daughter is becoming a woman. Not only Pique is changed. The log house on the river has been renovated. A large picture window permits Morag to look out onto the river while she is writing at her kitchen table. She has sold off most of the eighty acres but has kept some meadows and woodland.

Morag is perusing the reviews of *Shadow of Eden*. Most of them are good. A few bother her — but not as much as they used to when she was a beginning writer. At forty-four, Morag is realizing that she is now recognized as an established author. There is a new generation of Canadian writers, and she has become friends with several.

Pique is troubled. She asks her mother what the legal age is for quitting school in Ontario. Although Pique claims that she does not see the relevance of much that is taught in school, the real reason for her discontent soon emerges. Pique says students have been insulting her, calling her a "dirty halfbreed" and referring to Morag as a crazy woman who writes dirty books. Morag recognizes the old pattern — so similar to the ones that she and Jules had to endure as children. She tells Pique that she had hoped their child would never have to live through them.

Dinner passes in silence. Afterwards a truck pulls up outside. The visitor is Jules. He and Morag greet each other and kiss as old friends. When she calls him "Skinner," they both laugh. Jules says his brother Jacques is the only other person who calls him that. At forty-seven, Jules looks more like Lazarus than ever. His eyes are tough yet tired, his beer belly has increased and his hair is greyer and longer. Morag becomes aware that Jules is similarly appraising her. In a quiet voice he says they are both older.

Jules has come for one evening and night only. He wanted to see Morag and thought it time — after ten years — to see his daughter again. Pique, who has been watching them, interjects coldly that she knows who Jules is.

Morag gets him a beer. He does not apologize to Pique for his ten-year absence, nor does he defend himself. He tells her he is still singing, but he is getting older. Pique contradicts him, denying he is getting older — despite what her eyes tell her. Jules laughs and goes out to get his guitar. Morag thinks that Pique must want to tell him that she too is learning to play the guitar. She likes listening to solo singers who write their own songs.

Jules sings his song, which Pique can barely remember, about Old Jules Tonnerre. After he finishes, Pique just gives him a silent nod. Morag sees that, unlike her, both her daughter and Jules can speak without words. Jules tells them he has written a song about his father at last. The song he sings reveals to Pique many things she didn't know before. Jules is bitter and remarks that there is a lot Morag probably never told her.

After another beer, Jules sings a song about his sister, Piquette. The recurrent images of fire and snow in the lyrics suggests the life and death of Piquette. Morag and her daughter are silent at the end, not knowing what to say until Pique finally remarks simply, "It's a good song." Jules has not written of any others in his family, nor has he written about himself. However, he tells Pique about what happened to his brother, Paul, and of how his sister, Val, died, of "booze and speed, on the streets of Vancouver."

Pique is angry and bewildered, not understanding why her father had to tell her these things. Jules bangs the table and replies that too many have died, and he doesn't want her or himself to be among them. When Pique starts to cry, Jules lightly embraces her. He tells her of Jacques, the brother who has made a place for himself on Galloping Mountain. Pique should go to see him, Jules advises.

At this point, Jules shows Pique the only keepsake he has that belonged to his father. He pulls out a tarnished silver brooch from his wallet. Morag immediately recognizes it as a plaid pin and asks Jules how on earth Lazarus came by it. Jules replies that Lazarus had traded his knife to a boyhood friend of his for the pin. The friend, John Shipley, was killed in a head-on collision with a freight train before the war. Lazarus gave the pin to Jules after the war. Morag explains to Jules how John Shipley had sold his knife to Christie for a pack of cigarettes. Christie did not know who the real owner of the knife was when he gave it to Morag. Pique then goes upstairs and brings down the knife. She starts to give it to her father, hesitates, then gives it to Morag. Morag looks at the sign on the handle of the knife. She had always wondered about its significance, and now she sees that it is a sideways capital T. She gives the knife to Jules in exchange for the plaid pin.

Later, Morag looks through her copy of *The Clans and Tartans of Scotland*. She finds the pin is identified as that of the Clanranald Macdonalds. The book identifies the motto as *My Hope is Constant in Thee* and the war cry as *Gainsay Who Dare*.

She recalls that the Gunns do not have a crest or a coat-of-arms. She has adopted the crest of the Clanranald Macdonalds — as she has adopted before. The motto is filled with echoes from the past for her. It does not matter whose voice it is she hears. It matters only that she hears it. These words have been given to her: *Gainsay Who Dare*. Morag will not deny what has been given to her.

Commentary

The imagery of gardens recurs throughout this chapter and helps tie together several concerns which thread through the novel. Catharine Parr Traill cultivated her garden in the bush — her assertion of woman's power to give the land a human face. Morag lets her garden go to weed and delights in wildflowers. Now she can accept Nature just as she can increasingly accept human nature and all of the varieties found in that garden. The garden Morag cultivates is a literary one: she uses words to give the world a shape, an identity, a connection with human nature. Morag does not really know to which wildflowers the names relate. Pique knows that her mother simply loves the beauty of the names.

The third memorybank movie in this chapter is called "Shadow of Eden" — the title of Morag's fourth novel. Thus the theme of possession and dispossession is reintroduced.

Morag's novel deals with the dispossessed Sutherlanders who leave their home and native land, Scotland, never to return. They lose one Eden, wander through the wilds of Manitoba, then claim their shadow of the lost Eden in the Red River Valley. Similarly, Morag lost her Eden the day she left her first home, the farm near Manawaka, after her parents died. After that she wandered, searching for a home.

She finds that home in the first memorybank movie of Chapter 10, entitled "Beulah Land." This is the name given by John Bunyan in his *Pilgrim's Progress* (1666) to the land of peace. We are reminded of Morag's comment in Chapter 9 that "her need to make pilgrimages had led her back here" — to Canada, to the home she establishes on the river. An advertisement she reads in a Toronto newspaper about a pioneer farmhouse for sale near McConnell's Landing strikes her immediately. After seeing the farm, she intuitively knows it is for her. She will have ancestors, land, roots, "a place to stand and a place to grow." This epiphany releases her from the sense of ennui, the fear of the city and the hours spent sleeping to escape her depression. She experiences a new freedom as she embarks on her adventure of discovery. Morag's success as a novelist does not thrill her, but it provides her with the money to build solid foundations under her castle in the air. She will be a new — if compromised — pioneer.

Morag's novel *Shadow of Eden* is largely based on the stories Christie told her long ago. Telling the tales anew in her own voice, she is nonetheless following in his footsteps. The stories Jules told her that he had learned from his father are woven in too. In researching carefully the historical facts, Morag discovers that the fictional facts differ. That does not matter. She writes to Ella that she likes "the thought of history and fiction interweaving." She is beginning to understand the inner truths that Christie knew. Her discovery that Piper Gunn "probably never lived in so-called real life" does not bother her. He "lives forever" in the myths which she is now retelling. This feeling is echoed by Jules later in the chapter when he sings of his father: "Lazarus, oh man, you didn't die." And Morag realizes that, for Pique, who never met the "real" Christie, Christie never died because she knew him through Morag's tales. Those who "had their being once" live on in story and song. They give later artists a base from which to create.

Morag herself is becoming something of a mythical figure: Pique is perturbed by the local folklore which has tagged her mother as a crazy woman. Similarly when Jules arrives in McConnell's Landing, he has no trouble finding Morag's farm. Everyone knows where the "crazy woman" lives.

When Pique meets her father for the first time in ten years, she is fired by his songs and stories to know more about her "other side." The injustices of the past done to her Métis forebears can partially be vindicated by art — but only partially. When Jules tells her about how his brother Paul died under mysterious circumstances and how his sisters Val and Piquette died, he has another reason. "Too many have died," he tells her. "I don't aim to be one of them. And I don't aim for you to be neither." Ironically, he will kill himself only three years later. His daughter will have to recover him in song, in her own time, for future generations.

The last words of the chapter, "Gainsay Who Dare" is applicable to more than Morag. Those who gainsay or deny their past and their affinity to a larger community cannot be free.

Notes

alchemy: A magical, pseudo-scientific process of transmuting some common thing into gold. (p. 404)

Jacob wrestling with the Angel of the Lord: Symbolizes man struggling and being rewarded for his struggle by God. (See Genesis 32:24) (p. 410)

Carthage, Askelon, Babylon: Ancient cities in North Africa and the Middle East whose ruins still remain, they here symbolize civilizations which have been destroyed. (p. 410)

Daniel and the Lion's Den: Symbolizes a person whose faith in God enables him to survive despite the threat of seemingly inevitable destruction. (See Daniel 6:16-22) (p. 410)

Belshazzar's Feast: Symbolizes the imminent fall of evil, powerful rulers. In Daniel 5, while King Belshazzar is feasting, writing which appears on the wall, predicts he will fall because he has displeased God. (p. 410)

new heaven and new earth: From the book of Revelation (21:1-2). (p. 422)

Baez, Dylan, Cohen, Joni Mitchell, Buffy Sainte-Marie, James Taylor, Bruce Cockburn: Contemporary folk-singers, still popular, but particularly emblematic of the spirit of the late 1960s. (pp. 425-426)

Gainsay Who Dare: The war cry of the Clanranald Macdonalds. (pp. 432-433)

PART V • CHAPTER 11

Summary

It is now autumn: the Canada geese have flown south, the air is cold, and leaves are falling from the trees. Pique and Morag are drinking coffee together, and Pique is telling her mother about her visit to Manawaka. She went down to the valley where Jules and Lazarus had lived, and where her namesake, Piquette, had died in the fire. Pique is glad to have gone there. For the first time, she really sensed that the Tonnerre family lived there once. She also visited the cemetery where Christie and Prin were buried. Some flowers had been planted, and a weary, middle-aged woman was weeding the grave. Morag realizes that the woman would be Eva Winkler.

Pique then announces that she is going to travel out west again — this time to Galloping Mountain, where Jacques Tonnerre, his wife Mary, and numerous children live. She wants to take on the household chores and help care for the young ones. She feels a need to be part of this extended family, and has written to Jacques. Although Morag is worried about Pique's future, she decides to say simply that she hopes all will go well.

Then, for the first time, Pique sings one of her songs for Morag. It is about the valley and the mountain that hold her name, her search for her roots and her need to belong somewhere. Afterwards, mother and daughter sit silently until Morag reaches out to touch Pique's hand and ask for a copy of the lyrics.

That evening, Morag receives a telephone call from Jules' partner Billy Joe, who tells her that Jules is very ill with throat cancer. Morag knows she must leave for Toronto immediately.

The address Billy Joe has given her takes Morag to a decrepit rooming house in the core area of the city. Billy Joe greets her at the door and leads her to Jules' room. Morag is afraid of what she'll have to face: Jules is stretched out on the bed, cheaply dressed, his hair nearly as grey and as long as Morag's. His body is lean, eroded away, but he does not look sick. When Jules realizes that it is Morag, not Billy, in his room, he demands to know what she is doing there. Jules begins to cough and spit, but dismisses Morag's suggestion that he go into the hospital. He claims he's had some good luck in his time, but now it is over. Morag pours two stiff drinks. She sees the sweat on his forehead and around his mouth reflecting a physical pain she has never known and asks if he has any pills. He takes three and sinks back on the bed.

He hasn't sung for some time, but for the most part, he tells Morag, he has done what he wanted to do in life. Morag suddenly understands that she will never know what is going on in his mind and what pain he has known.

She reveals that Pique is going out to Galloping Mountain. Jules reaches for another drink and then faces her "with some residue of the ancient anger. . ." saying: "You let her be, see? You just let her be." Morag gives him her copy of Pique's song, and Jules regrets that he can't hear his daughter sing it, but forbids Morag to let Pique know he is sick.

Morag and Jules drink some more, exchanging few words. She turns off the light and the two of them sleep together, clothed, connected only by their hands and arms. Morag leaves in the morning before he awakens, knowing she will never see him alive again.

Back in her house on the river, four days later, Morag is unable to write. She has not told Pique about Jules nor suggested to her that anything is amiss. She recalls the silence surrounding the death of her father and mother and knows that Pique would want to know about Jules. Meanwhile, Pique is preparing to leave for Galloping Mountain.

That evening, Billy Joe arrives with the news that Jules has killed himself. He brings with him Jules' knife, to give to Pique, then embraces Morag silently and leaves. Morag telephones her daughter at the Smiths. When Pique comes home and sees the Tonnerre knife on the table, she realizes instantly that something has happened to her father. Morag tells her he died of throat cancer, and confesses that she had gone to Toronto to see Jules before he died. She had given him a copy of Pique's song and told him that Pique was planning to go to Galloping Mountain. Pique picks up the knife and Morag affirms that it is for her. Morag wonders if Pique will make a fiction out of Jules. Will she create "something both more and less true than himself, when she finally made a song for him, as she would someday, the song he had never brought himself to make for himself?"

A few days later, Pique heads out west again — this time by train. She bids her mother goodbye, and asks her if she can have the plaid pin. Morag has given it some thought, and has decided she needs it herself: "Not right now, Pique. It's some kind of a talisman to me. You can have it, though, when I'm through with it . . . . When I'm gathered to my ancestors." Pique grins in understanding. She hopes that won't be for a long time. Pique leaves, and, later that day, Morag hears the whistle of the train as it moves west.

In the days that follow, Morag is finally able to get back to work. One day she is interrupted by Royland, who usually avoids coming over during her working hours. He apologizes for the intrusion, but adds that maybe she won't mind this once. Royland looks the same as ever — but something is different. Morag pleads silently that nothing is wrong; too much has happened recently.

Royland informs Morag matter-of-factly that his divining powers have left him forever. Despite her suggestion that this is a temporary setback, Royland insists quite calmly that he has had the gift a long time and now he doesn't. It's as simple as that. Then he reveals something he had never hinted at before. Divining is something he does not understand; it's not something anyone can do, but it *can* be learned . . . by some people. A-Okay tried it, Royland says, but his skepticism got in the way. Nevertheless, A-Okay could learn, Royland believes, if he could just get over wanting to explain it. Morag pauses to reflect: "The inheritors. Was this, finally and at last, what Morag had always sensed she had to learn from the old man? She had known it all along, but not really known. The gift, or portion of grace, or whatever it was, was finally withdrawn, to be given to someone else."

Royland does not see it as a matter for mourning. Morag agrees. After he leaves, she sits beside her window, contemplating. Royland was a true diviner. She mentally compares his gift of divining, with her gift of creating things with words. She gets up, goes out and walks towards the river. It is near sunset on this fall day, and the river surface reflects the golden light. The river's current is visible, even though the wind blows the surface water in the opposite direction. Thus the river seems to be flowing both ways.

"*Look ahead into the past, and back into the future, until the silence.*" This thought flows through Morag's head. She wonders how far one can see into the river. Near its edge, clamshells and small live fish can be seen clearly. But farther away in the depths, the underwater life of the river is silent and invisible.

Commentary

Just as Part I of *The Diviners* is a single, short chapter, so is Part V. In this concluding chapter, all of the manifold threads of the novel are brought together. Laurence, however, does not impose artificial resolutions upon her complex characters and situations. As in life, many questions are left unanswered; the same pervasive sense of life's quirky and paradoxical nature we found in the opening chapter remains in the conclusion. As Morag earlier said, "Ambiguity is everywhere."

This is the only chapter of the novel set entirely in the continuing present, although it is written in the past tense. The last italicized thought of Morag is worth quoting here, for it reveals the sense of time, the quality of mind, and the paradoxical nature of the river which run throughout the book: *Look ahead into the past, and back into the future, until the silence.*

Life is essentially mysterious. It cannot be neatly analysed and broken down into its component parts, nor can we agree on one version, one interpretation or one way of seeing. We must be aroused out of our conventional ways of seeing, for we cannot see far into the river. Close at hand, some things are visible. But the hidden life is out of sight in the depths that we can only learn, through strength of conviction, to divine.

Notes

Spadina: Spadina Road is in west downtown Toronto, near the University. Jules' last home was in a rooming house on Spadina with Billy Joe. (p. 442)

Aeons: Eons, ages. (p. 447)

talisman: An object carried to bring good luck. Morag's plaid pin is a talisman to her. (p. 450)

shaman: A wise old man of the tribe who has special contacts with the divine. Royland is regarded by Morag as a shaman until he loses his powers, his gift to divine water. (p. 451)

102

Character Sketches

Morag Gunn

Morag Gunn herself is, of course, one of the diviners. In considering her character, we are really considering the whole novel, for every page reveals her to us.

Since Laurence uses the third person/first person narrative voice in telling the story, everything comes to us through the filter of Morag's perceptions, past and present. How reliable a source of information is she about herself and others? Examine the words and phrases she uses about herself, and note how many of them are questions. Morag is constantly examining herself.

When the novel begins and ends, Morag is forty-seven. Her mirror shows a tall woman, not fat, but heavier than when she was younger. Her somewhat leathery tanned face has strong, sharp features. Bushy eyebrows meet in the middle over dark brown eyes partly concealed by heavy-framed glasses. Her hair is long and straight. Once tar-black, it is now greying evenly. She is not vain about her appearance. "What kind of character am I?" she wonders. Morag's whole life is a pilgrimage to discover who she is and where she belongs. Questioning, self-examining, self-aware, she is constantly holding a mirror up to herself, and to her life. She is blessed — or cursed — with a good memory. In fact she seems to forget nothing. Her memorybank movies are packed with factual and fictional details which closely intertwine.

Inspired by the stories Christie tells her about her mythical ancestors, Morag starts writing while still a child. When her Grade Nine teacher recognizes her talent, Morag feels that a friendly but merciless hand has been placed on her shoulder: she must write and give vent to her inner voices that demand a life of their own on paper.

Morag continues to write throughout the years. She is committed, in her writing, to searching for — creating — some kind of order out of the elements of her life. The urge to write and to divine the truth — is strongly connected to this need to create order, to shape and give meaning to her experience. However, Morag is often frustrated in her work by the sense that the truth is eluding her — that words cannot adequately convey what she means.

Morag, who seeks to divine the truths of human nature, most interested in *character*. Much of her empathy with the dispossessed of the world comes from her own early experiences of being different. Morag can empathize with the Métis, particularly after she comes to know and love Jules Tonnerre, but she can never know first-hand what it is to *be* a Métis. As a writer she strives to understand, but is constantly hampered by the difficulties of understanding how it is for someone else. In one conversation with Ella Gerson she reflects on how she thought the work of writing would get easier. But it doesn't: as one gains in self-knowledge, one becomes even more aware of the complexities and profound individuality of human beings. Ultimately, Morag understands, there cannot be only one version of the truth.

Morag is involved not only in the lives of her characters, but also in the lives of her friends and, particularly, her daughter. When Pique leaves home, Morag is the one being left behind, just as she had left her adoptive parents years before. She worries about Pique, but knows better than to interfere. Pique must make her own way in the world, just as her mother did. Morag is keenly aware that there is a danger in seeing Pique's life as paralleling hers; they are similar, yet unique.

Here is Morag's — and Laurence's — greatest realization about freedom. We must respect the right of others to become themselves. If we try to reduce this to a formula, we may come up with something disturbingly bland and clichéd: we are all alike and yet different. Through the depiction of Morag and Pique we are given much more than mere truisms. We are shown two complex, ambiguous, strong women seeking to define themselves in the world.

Morag can see herself as a neurotic mother, always worrying, apologizing and feeling guilty. She also recognizes that she is a survivor. Like her mythical namesakes, Morag and Piper Gunn, Morag has a foundation of faith or, in Christie's words "strength of conviction."

At the end of the novel, when she dismisses her "mentor," the ghost of Catharine Parr Traill, Morag is confident. "I'm going to stop feeling guilty that I'll never be as hard-working or knowledgeable or all-round terrific as you were," she says. "And yet in my own way I've worked damn hard and I haven't done all I would've liked to do, but I haven't folded up like a paper fan either." This is an honest self-appraisal. Morag has come to terms with herself.

Even when she comes to feel that the gift of writing will be taken from her, she is neither bitter nor resentful. "The gift, or portion of grace, or whatever it was, was finally withdrawn, to be given to somebody else," she realizes. This is not a matter for mourning, but for acceptance.

Christie Logan

Christie Logan, seventy-six, is on his deathbed. Morag Gunn sits beside him, searching for the words she wants to say: "Christie — I used to fight with you a lot, Christie, but you've been my father to me." Christie's response is a whisper: "Well — I'm blessed." His eyes tell Morag that he has *chosen* those untypical words. So, at last, Morag has recognized her father in spirit.

Years earlier, Christie and his wife, Prin, took the orphaned Morag into their junk-laden home on Hill Street. Christie was the town garbageman, and young Morag felt ashamed of him, rejecting him.

While they certainly battled over the years, Christie never beat Morag. He once suggested that his epitaph should be *He Meant Well*. It is many years before Morag can acknowledge Christie the Scavenger as her first diviner and her real father. After his death, she writes Ella: "Christie knew things about inner truths that I am only just beginning to understand."

Christie's way with words is powerful. His language is always direct, yet allusive and ambiguous: raw and earthy, vulgar, exact and resonant — a reflection of the man himself. To appreciate the resonance of his language, one must read aloud his tales of Piper Gunn, his "By their garbage shall ye know them" speech and his alcohol-fuelled ramblings. Christie speaks honestly and prophetically. Echoes of Biblical prophets such as Jeremiah and Job reverberate in his burred tones.

While telling tales is his talent, seeing is Christie's specialty. Christie is an artist — a diviner who sorts through the junkyards of Manawaka and the debris of our linguistic, historical and mythical past. What Manawaka throws away to the Nuisance Grounds is his treasure. He reads garbage as he reads books: it reveals to him truths about the buried lives of the Manawakan townsfolk.

Manawakan society avoids Christie. He is no fool, but when children jeer at him in the street, he assumes the role, gibbering and drooling — to young Morag's mortification. He explains later that he is simply giving the audience what they want to see. If people are taken in by appearances, that is their problem.

Gaelic is a lost language to him — a language discarded by all but a few Scots and Irish. He does not know what the old words mean, but he loves their sounds and the suggestions of a glory that is passed from the earth. Christie, referring to the stories of his ancestral past, acknowledges that the "glory" probably never existed in the first place. But "We believe what we know," and what he knows are the old legends and myths of Scotland and Canada as it was in earlier days. He tells tales of Piper and Morag Gunn, ancestors he invents for Morag and how "there was no end to their suffering. But they didn't give in." By telling these stories, Christie gives Morag a connection with a namesake, a belief in "strength of conviction" and a sense of pride in the past. Also, he is inspiring her to become a story-teller, for, after hearing his stories, Morag starts to scribble down her own tales of the fabled ancestor Morag Gunn. Thus, Christie may be compared to the mythical figure of the wise old shaman, or bard, who taught other generations the myths and rituals of the community.

As he ages, Christie forgets the stories, but remembers telling them. He can still laugh his ironic laugh, even on his deathbed. His anger and rage against an unjust universe still burst forth, but his gentleness and kindness are always present.

Morag is Christie's inheritor. For part of her life, she rejects him and Manawaka. His smells, his seeming lack of ambition and his shabby house offend her. However, he is right when he prophesies that these memories will always remain with her. Years later, Morag realizes that Manawaka and Christie are the sources of all her art, wherever she may go. She has been shaped in Manawaka and by Christie. His words echo and live in her soul; his sayings become her proverbs. When Morag realizes that *home* for her means Christie's country and that the myths are her reality, she is paying tribute to her "real" father, whose name is an echo of "Christ" and whose function is that of diviner.

Jules "Skinner" Tonnerre

Jules "Skinner" Tonnerre: Morag can never properly pronounce his first name: it always came out as *Jewels*. "Jules" is the name of his forebear — a young man who fought in the last Métis uprising in the Northwest Rebellion of 1885. "Skinner" is his nickname at school: some say it is because he is a skinny kid; some maintain it is because he can skin any animal. Jules himself does not say. *Tonnerre* is French for "thunder" — and an undercurrent of thunder can be heard rumbling throughout the novel as a sort of repressed anger which only occasionally storms forth.

An outsider, Jules drifts in and out of the lives of Morag and his daughter Pique. He grew up in the shack community built by his father, Lazarus, in the Wachakwa valley outside the town of Manawaka. As children, he and Morag attend the same school. One of Morag's first recollections of the young Métis is of his silence during the singing of *The Maple Leaf Forever* — a song that does not mean much to him, since it tells nothing of his French-Canadian and Cree Indian heritage.

Jules and Morag exchange grins of recognition in school, sensing a kindred spirit. They meet in the Nuisance Grounds and down in the valley. There, when he is nineteen, and she sixteen, they eventually have sex together.

The following day, Jules leaves for the war. He survives Dieppe in 1942, but barely speaks of it when Morag sees him again three years later. In fact, Jules seldom speaks revealingly of himself. This will be left to Pique, the daughter who results from his union with Morag years later. Pique will continue Jules' tradition of singing the songs of the Métis people. Morag wonders if Pique will create a fiction out of her father, "both more and less true than himself. . . ." Certainly the mixture of myth and fact is strong in Jules Tonnerre.

While Jules and Morag are both outsiders who share experiences from time to time, he always reminds her that he is different. His consciousness of being Métis is strong; he never lets Morag forget she is white, and one of the people who ultimately dispossessed the Indians and still oppress them. Morag often senses that she can say nothing to him, incapable as she is of feeling his pain. Jules and Pique seem to understand without words — they need to talk far less than she.

When he was young Jules swore he would never be like his

father Lazarus. As he grows older, the resemblance grows more noticeable. At forty-seven, Jules has the tired, battle-worn eyes of an old man. His hair is long and grey, his face lined. He is bitter about the deaths of family members Val, Paul, Piquette and her two children, blaming the white society which cast them aside. His own decline he attributes to bad luck. After years of singing and drinking in bars with his friend Billy Joe, Jules finds he is dying of throat cancer. He takes death into his own hands quietly and with dignity, using the Tonnerre knife which Billy Joe subsequently hands over to Morag.

Unlike his father Lazarus or his surviving brother, Jacques, Jules never settles down to raise a family. He visits his one known daughter when she is five, fifteen and eighteen years of age. In spite of sharing only brief moments together, Pique and Jules share a bond — and Pique feels she "knows" her father.

Pique

"The valley and the mountain hold my name," sings Pique in her first song. But who is she? Born in Vancouver to Morag Gunn, her father is Jules Tonnerre. She is named after Jules' sister, Piquette, who died in a fire in the Wachakwa valley, but neither Morag nor Jules can bear to call her by her full name, so she is simply "Pique."

Pique is the inheritor of French-Indian and Scottish-Canadian roots. Raised by her mother in Canada and England, it is the Scottish-Canadian sensibility that dominates her early years. Although Morag has told her daughter tales of her Métis forebears, it is only when 15-year-old Pique meets her father for the second time that she hears from the other side, from the heart. Then she wonders if, through the years, she has been denied one part of herself.

Pique, at 18, is more mature than her mother was at the same age. Unlike young Morag, she does not seek to reject her heritage, but to explore both sides of it. Thus, she braids her hair, announcing to her mother that she is, after all, part-Indian. When she goes to Galloping Mountain where her Uncle Jacques has established his tribal home, she leaves without the bitterness Morag felt upon leaving Manawaka. Pique does not assign blame when she expresses her feelings in song or when she questions why her mother bore her. But she wants to know "what *really* happened." Like Morag, Pique is strong.

Although troubled by the racial and sexual slurs she is subjected to, she will not be put down. Pique learns to deal with power in her own ways. It took ten years for Morag to learn how to stand up to Brooke's chauvinism; we suspect that Pique would not tolerate such a situation in the first place. When she realizes she must leave Gord, and later, Dan, it is not without regret or caring. But she will not bind herself to a man at the sacrifice of her own being.

Like Morag, Pique is an explorer of territory, place, heritage and identity. She recognizes earlier than her mother that the search for a personal identity is connected to the search for place, for home, for a "tribe." Pique wants to discover what it is she must do with her life. By autumn, she thinks it will involve her Métis self and her songs. Yet she acknowledges that she doesn't have the gift of second sight and doesn't know if all will go well. "It will and it won't, I guess," she offers. A realist, Pique can accept the uncertainties of life.

Warm, open, honest and caring, Pique must find out who she is. She has a need for family, but not in the white traditional sense. Rather, it is more the extended family of the tribe that she wants to feel part of. Thus she leaves at the end of the novel for Galloping Mountain where her Uncle Jacques and Aunt Mary are raising their children. Pique's individuality is combined with a co-operative spirit, and it is to the community at Galloping Mountain that she feels she must make her contribution.

We see that in Pique is embodied much of Morag and of Jules. As a young girl she shared with her mother a fascination with words and a love of stories. Her repeated "what means. . .?" echoed Morag's early questions. When she is a teenager, songmaking passed down from Jules, becomes a part of her life. As she sings of "the voices that in me would never die," we hear an echo of her father's song about his father, Lazarus: "Oh man, you didn't die," sang Jules. The tales will live on in Pique's songs. We sense that, with her mixed heritage, she will take over from her forebears on both sides as a teller of tales, a singer of songs and a diviner of those things that won't die, but are passed on.

Royland
Royland is simply Royland to everyone. We never learn his last name. "Roi" is French for "king" — "King of the Land"

109

is thus the meaning of his bilingual single name. His simple dignity is further suggested by the titles given him by Morag: "Old Man River. Shaman. Diviner." His past life is suggested by the title he gives his former self: "Maverick."

Royland is a short-sighted man of seventy-four who is too stubborn to wear glasses, typically clad in denims and a plaid bush jacket, he is "large and bulky as a polar bear," and, because he will not bother to shave, has a grey beard which he keeps neatly trimmed.

He spends much of his time fishing. There is in mythology an old legend of a Fisher-King who presides over a wasteland whose barrenness is an extension of the old King's impotence and consequent sterility. Royland has no children, but Pique regards him as a grandfather, and the land in Southern Ontario where he finds water underground is fertile. Thus Royland is an original variation of the traditional mythical figure.

For a long time he does not talk much about his past. He divines more from Morag than she does from him. But he does let slip that he used to be a maverick — a non-conformist. One day she asks him to explain.

As a younger man, he says, he was a fiery preacher, arrogant, self-righteous and fanatical. Unaware that he was abusing his power, he lorded his knowledge of sin and the wrath of God over others. When his wife left him, he went after her and promised to change, to be more tolerant, understanding and caring, and to settle down. She, still terrified of him, committed suicide.

This changed Royland's life completely. Shaken by the experience, he travelled up north and worked in lumber camps for five years, purging himself. He came to see that he had been "crazy as a loon before" in his proud, fanatical ways.

When he learned how to divine water — he never explains how — he decided it was better to find water than to raise fire. He turned his life towards helping rather than damning others. Royland confesses to Morag that, while he has not believed in hell for years, he has lived through it on earth.

Through his suffering, Royland has divined wisdom. And he can divine water through a process he has never understood nor sought to understand. "I just gotta do it," he declares. He sees no value in worrying, and counsels Morag to be less hard on herself. He can speak of guilt, suffering and hardship because he has known them himself.

Eventually, he says that A-Okay could learn to divine water if he would just stop seeking for a scientific explanation of how it is done. "But that's up to him," he says. Royland no longer seeks to impose his views on others.

When he discovers he can no longer divine water himself, he is shaken but not resentful. Matter-of-factly he tells Morag that when he started with his willow wand to look for underground water one day, he knew somehow that nothing would happen. He doesn't find it strange. The gift was his for a long time, and now it is no longer his. "It is not a matter for mourning," he says, but for simple acceptance.

Morag felt for a long time that she would learn something of great significance from Royland. Perhaps this is it: the gift, the portion of divine grace, is ours only for a while. Our talents are God-given for us to use, but we do not possess them forever. Royland then reveals his secret: one *can* learn to divine. The gift *can* be, and is, transmitted to others, so that it does not die, but lives on.

Practical, kind, easy-going, tolerant and accepting, Royland cannot be reduced to a mere symbol. However, he does symbolize the shaman or wise old man so often found in literature. With his "ancient myopic eyes" he has insight into hidden sources of water and human wisdom, and is thus a true shaman and diviner.

Catharine Parr Traill

Catharine Parr Traill (1802-1899), like her well-known sister Susanna Moodie, was an English gentlewoman who settled in the bush near Peterborough, Ontario, in 1832. Mrs. Traill wrote several books on the plants and flowers and the pioneer life in what was then called Upper Canada.

The historical Mrs. Traill captures the imagination of Morag Gunn when the latter settles in the area pioneered by Moodie and Traill some 137 years earlier. Morag conjures up the spirit of C.P.T. (as she often calls her) to talk with — much to the amusement of Royland, who sometimes overhears Morag conversing out loud with her imaginary friend.

A *foil* is a character held up to reflect the characteristics of a major character. By juxtaposing the two characters, the author can better bring out, by means of comparison and contrast, the essentials of that major character: Laurence uses Traill

111

as a foil for Morag; indeed, Morag uses Traill as a foil for herself. Through her reflections on, and imaginary conversations with Mrs. Traill, the "new pioneer" measures her own self and her own development "roughing it in the bush" near McConnell's Landing.

Mrs. Traill wrote and survived as Morag trusts to write and survive. But, through most of the summer and fall Morag spends by the river, she is overawed by the legendary determination, activity, perseverance and formidable calm of her spiritual ancestor.

This larger-than-life woman, who could cook breakfast for "a multitude," feed the chickens, pull fourteen armloads of weeds, teach the children, bake "two hundred loaves of delicious bread" and preserve a half-ton of fruit "All before lunch," is obviously too much for any mere mortal to compete with. But this superwoman is a mythical being (like Morag's namesake, Piper Gunn's woman) and largely of Morag's own invention. The myth has replaced the historical being as the reality for Morag. Mrs. Traill has been transformed into "Saint Catharine" and this "saint" humbles and intimidates Morag.

Mrs. Traill symbolizes reason, order, control, activity. Morag comes to see that there was little room for feelings, for the irrational, in Mrs. Traill's neatly-organized world. By the autumn, Morag can summon up the ghost she has caused to haunt her — and dismiss her.

Morag's dismissal of Catharine Parr Traill is her dismissal of her last colonial overseer. She declares her independence of the tyranny of others, of the dead hand of the past, of her own inhibiting mythifications.

The words of Mrs. Traill which most haunt Morag are these: "In cases of emergency, it is folly to fold one's hands and sit down to bewail in abject terror. It is better to be up and doing." Even after Morag has dismissed Mrs. Traill, she still echoes this sentiment: "The necessary doing of the thing — that mattered." Morag has grown up to be able to reject what is harmful and to choose what is vital for her own survival.

Literary Elements

Diction and Prose Style

Diction is one's *choice* of words. The manner in which the particular words are combined constitute a writer's prose style.

Laurence chooses her words carefully from the four levels of word usage: formal, informal, colloquial and slang. When appropriate she uses archaic words such as "gainsay" and foreign words such as "dhu." She records the eloquent and the banal, the precise and the sloppy, the formal and the vulgar. Often her characters do not speak in complete sentences. They interrupt themselves and others. They wander in speech and revise their words — just as we speak in real life. Brooke is formal and precise in his diction and authoritarian in his style. Eva is awkward, imprecise and ungrammatical in hers. Each has a distinctive voice. Try to imagine Christie saying "darn" or Fan Brady using the expression "making love." The diction of the characters — the way they express themselves — is part of their being.

Like Laurence, Morag Gunn is a writer and is fascinated by words — particularly the relationship between a word and what it refers to. She wonders how flies can be given the nice name of *bluebottles* when they are so ugly; she finds it hilarious that *Princess* should be the real name of the grotesquely fat Prin. Choosing the "right" words to convey to another what one sees, feels and thinks, is difficult. Pique is frustrated by Morag's concern for the right word when she asks if her mother *loved* Jules. Although Pique wants a direct and simple answer to this question, Morag is caught up by the connotations and associations of the word "love:" "I guess you could say love. I find words more difficult to define than I used to." Morag had once felt that words could perform miracles, and express great truths, but comes to believe that they can only sometimes work their magic.

As an example of language used masterfully and magically, Laurence's description of the flight of the Great Blue Heron is worth close examination. It is poetic not only in its diction, but in its patterning, its musical cadences and rhythms, and its care for sound values. The heron takes off "like a pterodactyl, like an angel, like something out of the world's dawn." The initial hard sounds — "k," "pt," "c" — convey the sense of the

113

stacatto flapping of wings, while the drawn-out "a" in *angel* and the long vowel sounds in *out* and *dawn* suggest the flight of the bird as it soars high and glides away. Morag and Royland, out on the river in the evening, are transported by this vision, as the reader is transported by the poetry of the passage.

Paradox and Ambiguity

"The river flowed both ways." The opening statement of the novel is a paradox, a situation or statement which *seems* to be a contradiction. But, when we explore a paradox, we may discover that it is explicable. The current of the river is flowing from north to south. The prevailing wind is blowing from the south, thus rippling back the surface waters in the direction contrary to the current. Thus the river seems to be doing two things mutually opposite at the same time. Laurence plays with this initial paradox throughout the book. On the final page, the paradox is expressed differently: *Look ahead into the past, and back into the future, until the silence.* All is in process, all is changing, yet all remains the same.

Laurence has spoken of her ambition "to present the living individual on the printed page, in all his paradox and all his craziness." Morag wants to stay with the dying Christie and not to stay. How can she feel both ways at the same time? And how can she then call him "father" when her father was Colin Gunn? The paradox may be resolved if we delve below the surface material appearance: We have spiritual dimensions; Christie has in fact been a father *in spirit* to Morag.

Paradox leads us into *ambiguity*. We say that a person, a word, or a situation is ambiguous when it is capable of being validly interpreted in more than one way. Phrases such as "Maybe. Or maybe not," "Perhaps. Or perhaps not," "What *really* happened?" are ambiguities which echo throughout *The Diviners*. They create problems only if we believe that there has to be *one* truth, *one* reality, *one* interpretation. A large measure of the value of Laurence's writing is that she helps us to see with the eyes of others, to break out of our merely private understandings and to respect the views of others who may see and think and feel differently from ourselves. The world *is* ambiguous — much more so than fiction, Laurence asserts. As Morag says, "ambiguity is everywhere."

Description and Imagery

Laurence has written that she wishes her descriptions to be as sharp and instantaneous as possible. They should be brief, she says, because she perceives life as being caught in a series of sharp visual images which are fleeting. As an example, consider the description of Royland:

> Royland came to the door, looking old as Jehovah. Wearing his plaid wool bush jacket and heavy denims — a wonder he didn't melt. Greybeard loon . . . . Large and bulky as a polar bear, he filled the doorway.

Laurence's picture tells less than it suggests. We read that Royland is old, big, grey-bearded, dressed in heavy clothes. But he is old "as Jehovah." This suggests he is like the God of the Old Testament, an appropriate image for a character who is portrayed as a diviner and wise. The prosaic description of his dress must be correlated with the knowledge that it is a hot day: he seems resistant to the heat, almost supernatural. "Greybeard loon" is an allusion to Coleridge's "Ancient Mariner" — a character who suffered much in life and grew in wisdom. "Loon" suggests that some think him crazy. It may also remind us of the bird of Canada's northern lakes, a connection between his nature and Nature. The simile "Large and bulky *as* a polar bear" and they hyperbole or exaggeration in "he filled the doorway" suggest a larger-than-life figure, someone more than a mere man. All of these suggestions are supported by the total picture we get of Royland through Morag's admiring eyes throughout the novel. *The Diviners* is full of detailed writing like this, descriptions of people, things and events which on one level seem rich in visual detail, but are in fact deeply significant to the overall thematic and character presentations of the novel.

Imagery can refer to literal, sensory images in passages of description, but imagery in the sense of patterns or clusters of images may reveal other levels of meaning. Some critics see these patterns of images as being the basic meaning of a work. They believe such imagery, which is created subconsciously, provides a sounder key to interpretation than explicit statements by the author or elements of plot. Images of sight and insight and short-sightedness, for example, suggest some of the deepest sources of Laurence's imagination as revealed in *The Diviners*.

115

Imagery can also refer to the figures of speech, the non-literal images in a work. Laurence is sparing in her uses of similes and metaphors. Frequently Morag rejects a simile or metaphor as being inexact. For example, "The river was the colour of liquid bronze this morning, the sun catching it. Could that be right? No. . . .Probably no one could catch the river's colour even with paints, much less words."

Symbolism

A symbol is something which is itself and simultaneously stands for, or suggests, something else. Often it is something in the physical, sensuous world which comes to mean something abstract.

"The river of now and then" is clearly the most prevalent symbol in *The Diviners*. Laurence says that she interpreted the Otonabee River, which flows by her cottage, as a "natural symbol." In the book, the river is nameless and is thus better able to be *all* rivers and to represent that which is abstract. The river symbolizes time and memory, as suggested by its epithet, "now and then" and by the fact that the river, time, memory, all flow both ways. Laurence opposes the common view of a simple, single, linear flow from past through present into the future.

Manawaka is based on Laurence's home town of Neepawa, Manitoba. But Manawaka is definitely an *invention*, and it symbolizes all small towns. Laurence has said that Manawaka is a microcosm — a world in miniature — and that it contains all "the seeds of both man's freedom and his captivity" that one can find in the larger world.

Characters can also act as symbols, although it would be unfair and unwise to reduce any of Laurence's characters to *mere* symbols. However, Brooke Skelton is a symbol of the male chauvinist who must always have the upper hand; similarly, Chas symbolizes the unfeeling sexual tyrant. The Sutherlanders and Métis are representative of the dispossessed peoples of the world.

There are many other people, places, and things in the novel which have symbolic value. Symbols can act as a suggestive shorthand to summon up more than is literally there. But one must be careful not to reduce the richness of Laurence's symbolic harvest to a list of crude mechanical equivalences.

Cinematic Techniques

It is not surprising that film and television should have an influence on twentieth-century writers. Laurence has employed several devices from cinema in composing and structuring *The Diviners*.

Much of Morag's story is related through "memorybank movies," which tell, in the present tense, of the events of her earlier life. They are all flashbacks, sequentially ordered in her mind. They are highly visual, aural, and dramatic in content. In each case, something in the present sets off the first movie in each chapter. In Chapter Nine, for example, Morag is thinking that "her quest for islands had ended some time ago. . . ." This thought triggers the film appropriately titled "Sceptr'd Isle" and set in England. The second movie in that chapter, "The Black Isle," follows Morag's journey from England to Scotland. The third and last movie follows Morag's journey back to Canada for the death and funeral of Christie, whose clan's motto is the title of that movie: "The Ridge of Tears." Thus this last film of the chapter completes the original thought (the ". . . quest for islands had ended. . .") which had triggered the triology of films: ". . . and her need to make pilgrimages had led her back here."

The first movies in Chapter 1 are initiated by six "Snapshots," which are of moments frozen in time — static "freeze frames." What we see is what we get: a purely visual image lacking action and dialogue. Morag sees what the pictures *don't* show: she recalls and literally recreates what she remembers about that time in her life. She notes later that "everyone is constantly changing their past, recalling it, revising it." So it is not surprising that selection, editing and refilming, goes on with these snapshots and memorybank movies.

Snapshots of Pique are used in the eighth chapter, showing Pique frozen in time at the beginning of each of four movies dealing with her early years. This parallelism suggests the similarity between mother and daughter. Pique's pictures are in colour, however, where Morag's were in black-and-white.

The strict chronological sequence of the snapshots and movies has struck some critics as "clumsy" and "contrived." But we are told that order "flowed in Morag's veins, despise it as she might." The sequence is thus consistent with the nature of the director and star — Morag Gunn. If we follow the suggestions

117

of some critics that the movies are actually the plot of the novel Morag is writing in the present, the arrangement seems necessary.

Occasionally, Laurence uses what she calls *Innerfilms*. As the name suggests, they are films within films, picturing Morag's past fantasies in a tentative format. They are in the present progressive tense, briefly flashing by, being refilmed.

Morag often perceives the fluidity of life and memory in terms of film. She speaks of a sleepless night when "long and stupendously vivid scenes unfolded" and of how she "couldn't shut off the projector for the night. . . ." Films begin again in her imagination as an almost automatic process. "She could not even be sure of their veracity, nor guess how many times they had been refilmed, a scene deleted here, another added there. But they were on again, a new season of the old films." This reminds us that we are not dealing with strict documentaries, but with art, and thus with the literally "artificial." Film, the novel, the human mind, all are active and creative media.

Allusion

An allusion is a brief reference to something usually outside the literary work itself. Laurence makes many allusions, many of which are explained in the *Glossary* for these Notes. Her allusions are frequently to history, myth, other literary works — and occasionally to her other Manawaka books. The allusions to the plaid pin and the Shipley family at the end of Chapter 10, for example, are to Laurence's first Manawaka book, *The Stone Angel*. Allusions to Prospero and Miranda reach back to Shakespeare's *The Tempest* and relate *The Diviners* to the larger world of Western Culture.

Theme: The Quest For Freedom

The very questions "What is a theme?" and "What are Margaret Laurence's themes?" are themselves debatable. The reader must read carefully and reflect conscientiously to determine Laurence's concerns in *The Diviners*.

First, *theme* may be defined as a subject explored by the writer or the motif upon which the writer plays variations. In this primary sense, a number of themes are introduced in Chapter 1 of *The Diviners* and sustained throughout the novel. Among them are: freedom; survival; words; the presence of the past; possession and dispossession; the quest; the interweaving of fiction and history; creation and recreation; and divining.

The second literary meaning of *theme* is the central idea or statement the author makes in the work. Here one is on even shakier ground than before. However, it is perhaps safe to say that the first and last sentences of Chapter 1 make this kind of statement. Statements which leap out at the reader such as "The myths are my reality" also make thematic statements.

"The quest for physical and spiritual freedom, the quest for relationships of equality and communication — these themes run through my fiction," Margaret Laurence has written. This quest is intimately connected, particularly in *The Diviners*, with the themes of survival and the presence of the past. Laurence notes that freedom is gained through coming to terms with one's past and surviving. Freedom, she says, is "the ability to act out of one's own self-definition with some confidence and with compassion, uncompelled by fear or by the authority of others. . . ." Survival is not to be seen as mere physical endurance — although that is primary. It must involve "some human dignity and, in the end, the survival of some human warmth and ability to reach out and touch others. . . ."

We must recognize that the past is present in us. If we do not, we may be at the mercy of forces working within and against us, the dead hands of the past manipulating and controlling us without our knowledge. If we assimilate the past, we can be freed to recognize "its true value . . . a determination to survive against whatever odds," she writes. Laurence makes clear that this applies not only to individuals but to nations and it has particular reference to Canadians.

This double concern for individuals and communities

grows as Morag grows in maturity. At first she is primarily concerned for her own freedom — to get out of Manawaka on her own terms. The confining nature of small towns, particularly their hypocrisy and pettiness, has long been a theme in Canadian Literature. The seeming thrill of freedom, of the escape to a world of larger horizons, is often symbolized by the plaintive wail of the train, as it is for Morag.

Winnipeg and university symbolize freedom for Morag. But once in Winnipeg, she hears the Canada geese flying south and feels she is not yet far enough away. She will not go south to the United States, but instead travels to Toronto, Vancouver, England and Scotland before she is able to recognize that she must create her own home in Canada and there gain her freedom.

The freedom Morag seeks is not only physical freedom. It is also freedom of the spirit. She thinks she is free when she marries Brooke, but she is not. Perhaps she is misusing her freedom in marrying him; she escapes Manawaka, only to be enslaved by Dr. Skelton, who wants her to deny her past and accept the imposition of his needs upon her. Dispossessed of his own past, he clings to the illusion that Morag is his possession. It takes Morag years to realize that she *must* be free. For her to survive spiritually — to be free to be herself — she must leave him.

Brooke is a true imperialist. Laurence recognizes the degree to which the position of women often is like the position of colonies: where there is no respect for the rights of others, for the realities of others or for the equality of others, a smothering colonialism exists which is ultimately no good for either party.

In contrast to the chauvinistic colonizer Brooke, there are Morag's two other lovers — Jules and Dan. Jules and Morag respect each other, and share moments in their lives without demanding explanations. Dan and Morag also respect each other, as persons and as artists. They do not seek to possess each other or to impose their own identities or illusions of power on the other. Dan and Jules enjoy free and equal relationships with Morag, and their relationships survive, unaffected by apparent gaps in space and time.

Finally, Morag frees herself from the spirit of Catharine Parr Traill. She originally summoned up C.P.T. as her mentor; by the end of the book Morag finds that Mrs. Traill's ideas of order and control are inhibiting rather than inspiring. Morag dismisses her, and at last becomes what Margaret Atwood in her classic study of Canadian Literature, *Survival*, calls "a creative non-victim." Morag does not seek to blame others for the predicaments she finds herself in; rather, she accepts responsibility for her own fate. It is through her own strength, the grace of God and the divine gift of divining inner truths with her pen, that she finds freedom.

Selected Criticisms

The Diviners is a large and complex book, an orchestration of themes as well as a collection of stories. It is about Canada as well as Manitoba, "about the need to give shape to our own legends, to rediscover what is really ours, what is *here.*" Paradoxically, *The Diviners* is at once the most international of Laurence's books and the most national. "They are not," she says, "mutually exclusive."

Margaret Atwood, "Face to Face" in *Margaret Laurence*
(Ed. William New.) (McGraw-Hill Ryerson, 1977), p. 39.

. . . *The Diviners* joins the increasing number of Canadian novels of the seventies that explore the personal development of the artist . . . . Such portraits of the Canadian writer are a testimony to the self-consciousness and maturity of Canadian fiction."

David Staines, Introduction to *The Diviners*, (New
Canadian Library edition), p. xi.

Out of her daily round and the tangle of her memories, out of the tension between now and then, (Morag) composes a world that sometimes rises to eloquence, and *every now and then* descends to the banal, and otherwise records the different reaches of the Canadian English tongue. That there should be this unevenness of diction does not seem to me a flaw, but instead a deliberate effect: the novelist-author forcing the novelist-character to explore the limits of her verbal understanding, so that in turn the reader might learn the connection between mode of speech and pattern of thought.

William H. New, *Canadian Literature*, (Summer 1982), p. 79.

The Diviners is like a nest of Chinese boxes, stories within stories. Beginning with *Spear of Innocence*, Morag is remembering, writing, living, and turning her living into writing all at the same time . . . . The achievement of this novel lies in its technique; not in its theme. The emphasis is on tales in the telling: this gerund denotes not a completed structure but a continuous action.

Ildikó de Papp Carrington, *Essays in Canadian Writing,*
(Winter 1977-78), pp. 160, 168.

We finally have in Morag a feminine counterpart of Odysseus. She carries a lot more burdens than he does, including the whole metaphysical baggage of the twentieth century, but she comes home more surely and enduringly than he. Morag constellates a new archetypal feminine . . . As an American, I am curious as to what in Canadian culture is producing women writers like Laurence . . . . I think Margaret Laurence's body of literature will takes it place among that of the great women writers of all time like Jane Austen, Colette, and Virginia Woolf. She is revisioning what it means to be a woman, and her heroines are changing the very structure of characterization in world literature.

Stephanie A. Dematrakopoulos, Canadian Literature,
(Summer 1982), pp. 52, 55.

Laurence herself has called *The Diviners* "a very Canadian book." Some Canadians, however, have found it an unsettling mirror image, attributable, in part, to the fact that Morag is a woman who succeeds without a man. . . .

Sherrill Grace, Journal of Canadian Studies, (Autumn 1978), p. 70.

Toronto critics . . . are terrified of the monumental, particularly in the works of women. . . . *The Diviners* is not, it is true, as neat a book as *A Bird in the House*. There are signs in the text of blots and erasures, spilled ink, thumb-prints and tears. Tut, Tut, Ms. Laurence, girls should be neat. It is unladylike to achieve apocalypse.

Marian Engel, Journal of Canadian Studies, (Autumn 1978), p. 74.

Bibliography

Hind-Smith, Joan. "Margaret Laurence" in *Three Voices*. Toronto: Clarke, Irwin, 1975

Laurence, Margaret. *Heart of a Stranger*. Toronto: McClelland and Stewart, 1976. (Also available as a 1980 Bantam-Seal paperback)

Morley, Patricia. *Margaret Laurence*. Boston: Twayne, 1981

New, William, ed. *Margaret Laurence*. Toronto: McGraw-Hill Ryerson, 1977

Sorfleet, John R., ed. *The Work of Margaret Laurence*. Montreal: JCF Press, 1980

Thomas, Clara. *The Manawaka World of Margaret Laurence*. Toronto: McClelland and Stewart, 1976

Warwick, Susan J. "A Laurence Log," *Journal of Canadian Studies*, Vol. 13, No. 3 (Autumn 1978), pp. 75-83